THE **KAYAKING** HANDBOOK

Dagger

THE **KAYAKING** HANDBOOK

A BEGINNER'S GUIDE

BILL MATTOS

CONSULTANT: ANDY MIDDLETON

APPLE

This edition published in the UK in 2012 by
Apple Press
7 Greenland Street
London NW1 0ND
www.apple-press.com

ISBN: 978-1-84543-296-6

This book was designed and produced by
Anness Publishing Ltd
Blaby Road
Wigston
Leicestershire LE18 4SE
www.annesspublishing.com

PUBLISHER'S NOTE

Although the advice and information in this book are believed to be accurate and true at the time of going to press, neither the author nor the publisher can accept any legal responsibility or liability for any errors or omissions that may have been made nor for any inaccuracies nor for any loss, harm or injury that comes about from following instructions or advice in this book.

The author and publisher wish to stress that they strongly advise the use of a helmet and flotation aid in all paddling situations. There is no legal requirement to wear either, but paddling is all about taking responsibility for your own decisions, actions and personal safety.

CONTENTS

"There is nothing – absolutely nothing – half so much worth doing as simply messing about in boats." That's what Ratty said to Mole in Kenneth Grahame's beloved 1908 novel, *The Wind in the Willows*. "In or out of 'em, it doesn't matter. Nothing seems really to matter, that's the charm of it", Ratty continued.

"You must be curious about what lies beyond the envelope of your ability, and you must have an appetite for it."
Jim Snyder

"A C2 is a canoe paddled by two people who constantly scream at each other. A C2 paddled by a married couple is usually referred to as a D-I-V-O-R-C-E boat."
William Nealy

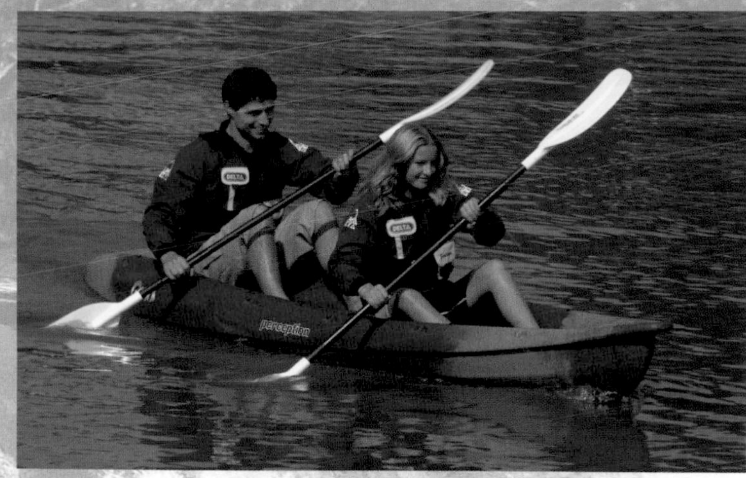

"For to boat, perchance to flip – aye, there's the rub."
William Nealy

"If there is paddling to be done, go and do it – you can read about it another time."
Richard Fox

"Before you get serious about canoeing, you must consider the possibility of becoming totally and incurably hooked on it."
Bill Mason

INTRODUCTION

Taking Up Paddling

The words "canoeing" and "kayaking" describe two similar but different types of small boat paddling. Collectively, they represent an activity that has a longer history than people now imagine, predating the invention of the wheel.

Thousands of years ago, primitive peoples hollowed out logs to make vessels for hunting, fishing and transport. Others such as the Inuit found ways to make boats from skins, bones, and driftwood. As they fashioned these simple craft, they could have no idea that they were developing designs for today's paddlers, or that their craft would one day be executed in space-age materials.

While canoeing and kayaking have existed for millennia, it was only during the recreation explosion of the twentieth century that these paddle sports experienced a meteoric rate of growth. It has touched the lives of the thousands of people who enjoy the outdoors, and in particular, the unrivalled pleasure of simply messing about in boats.

Spirit of Adventure

There is something about the simplicity of paddling a boat with a free blade – that is, a paddle unattached to the boat – that captures the imagination. Few who have tried paddling can deny that it is amazing fun, and that you can get a real sense of freedom even if it is your very first day on the water. Best of all is the fact that, providing you know the limits of your ability and have a responsible attitude towards personal safety, you don't need expert knowledge or any specialist skills to enjoy yourself.

Once you have dabbled at paddling for a while, you will start to get restless when you are away from the water for any length of time. In the words of the late Bill Mason, American canoe guru and author of many inspirational texts on the subject, "Before you get serious about canoeing, you must consider the possibility of becoming totally and incurably hooked on it." What first starts out as fun can quickly become addictive.

Children don't always concentrate on correct grip or posture – they're too busy having fun! These two are warmly dressed, correctly equipped, and having a fine time.

With the right boat and equipment, a day on the water will be a relaxed and happy affair.

How to Use This Book

The purpose of this book is to provide the beginner with a lively and accessible guide to taking up kayaking and canoeing, and is a seminal reference work for anyone who cares about making the most of their early paddling experience in a kayak or a canoe.

We will look at the best way to prepare yourself for paddling in order to have fun and to avoid taking risks. There is advice on choosing a suitable boat, and on getting the best from your gear and from your body. The essential equipment you will need for comfort, safety and performance is covered in detail, as are the physical skills and strokes which are described in depth to enable you to understand and master them with practice. These are covered in the order in which you are likely to need them, so that you can work your way through this section over time.

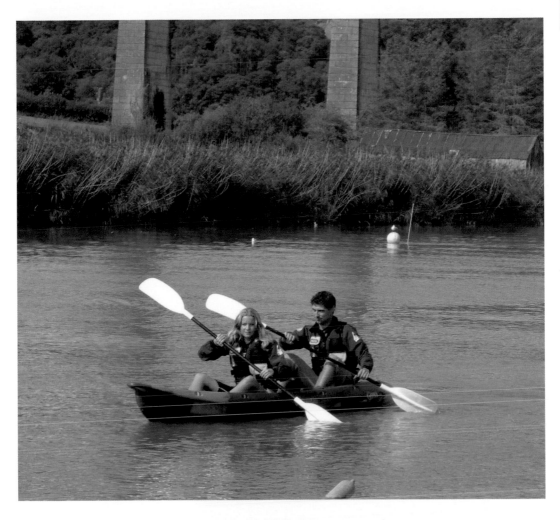

The emphasis is on helping you to make decisions and acquire skills safely and responsibly. There is also detailed information on safety and first aid issues that any paddler should know about.

Although you will undoubtedly benefit from reading this book right through before you try canoeing or kayaking, it is designed to be the sort of book you can continue to refer to as you progress. You should of course be aware of the basic do's and don'ts before you take to the water, and of the safety issues involved that may affect you. But don't feel that the theory is more important than the practice. There is nothing like time on the water – get paddling!

Two paddlers in a sit-on kayak making smooth and harmonious progress.

A kayaker enjoying bright sunshine and calm seas – the perfect conditions for a day on the water.

The Origins of Paddling

The design and appearance of kayaks and canoes have undergone a revolution since trees were first hollowed out by early tribesmen. Today's models are fast and lightweight, and tough enough to survive the most extreme water conditions.

Kayaking and canoeing share the same goal – to propel a craft over water by the simplest and most versatile means possible. Unlike rowing, there is an almost unbroken tradition in which the paddler faces the direction of travel, and this has helped make paddling a more versatile way of negotiating difficult water and overcoming changeable conditions. Rowing, on the other hand, is often a more efficient way of powering your way across water but, except in a race or a long journey across open water, power is worth little without the control provided by a free blade and a clear view ahead.

Canoe design developed out of need. Here, Native Americans use a dugout canoe to transport fresh fruit to store.

This painting shows an English ship meeting hostile natives on land and in kayaks in the waters off Greenland.

Early Boats

The first canoes were logs, paddled by hand or propelled with makeshift poles made from strong, stout branches. It can not have taken early tribes long to realize that a better and more stable alternative was a hollowed-out log. Depending upon the type of trees and tools available, the log was either scraped out or had a fire lit on top, burning out a hollow. There is archaeological evidence of both techniques. The one big problem with a craft fashioned from a solid log was the difficulty of transporting the heavy craft over land for any distance.

Kayak and Canoe Design

Eventually, people acquired the necessary tools and skills to construct a more manageable boat from scratch, using a variety of smaller components, and this is when the now distinct and quite separate forms of kayak and canoe first appeared.

The kayak was invented by the aboriginal Inuit peoples of the Arctic and sub-Arctic regions, probably because a single blade could not generate enough power in the rough seas in which the Inuit hunted and travelled. The kayak paddler, who always sits, uses a paddle with a blade at each end. A shortage of large pieces of wood or bone meant that ancient kayak paddles would have been shorter and thinner than they are today.

The canoe was developed in response to the needs of the native peoples of North America several thousand years ago. The boat is propelled using a single-blade paddle or a pole that is not attached to the boat, in which the paddler sits or kneels facing the direction of travel.

Inuit kayaks and North American canoes were first made from wood bark and bone frames with animal skins stretched over them. In other parts of the world, canoes resembled dugouts made from solid wood, except in South-east Asia, where bamboo was sometimes used.

Recreational Boats

Both kayaks and canoes were conceived out of necessity, and their form continued to follow their intended function. One of the first examples of a boat created purely for recreation was that of John MacGregor, nicknamed Rob Roy, a nineteenth-century English adventurer. MacGregor built his kayak in order to tour the inland waterways of Europe. His book, *A Thousand Miles in the Rob Roy Canoe*, may be the prime reason why many people still use the word "canoe" as a generic term for kayak or canoe. He designed his boat to fit in a railway carriage for easy transportation – modern kayaks are often small enough to fit into a family car!

John MacGregor's kayak, the Rob Roy. The boat was made using the clinker construction of traditional boatbuilding.

MacGregor encounters a herd of cattle swimming a river.

A Thousand Miles in the Rob Roy Canoe by John MacGregor. The illustration shows the author seated and using a two-bladed paddle: his craft is therefore a kayak, despite the book's title.

MacGregor gets a rapturous welcome from the Swiss town of Bremgarten.

The Evolution of Kayaks and Canoes

For thousands of years the basic form of kayaks and canoes changed little, but 200 years ago came the introduction of modern materials, including mass-produced woven fabrics and smooth-planed wood. While there are still a few Inuit hunting boats made from sealskins, the traditional boats have now been superseded.

In an effort to create lighter boats in the nineteenth and twentieth centuries, boats were given a canvas skin over a wooden frame. Light fold-up frames, such as the Klepper, were designed for easy transportation. While some canoes from the Victorian era made from wood construction methods, such as clinker (overlaying planks and/or woodstrip), have survived, the more common canvas boats of that time have not. Further changes came when the skins of kayaks and canoes were replaced by newer manmade fabrics, such as plywood.

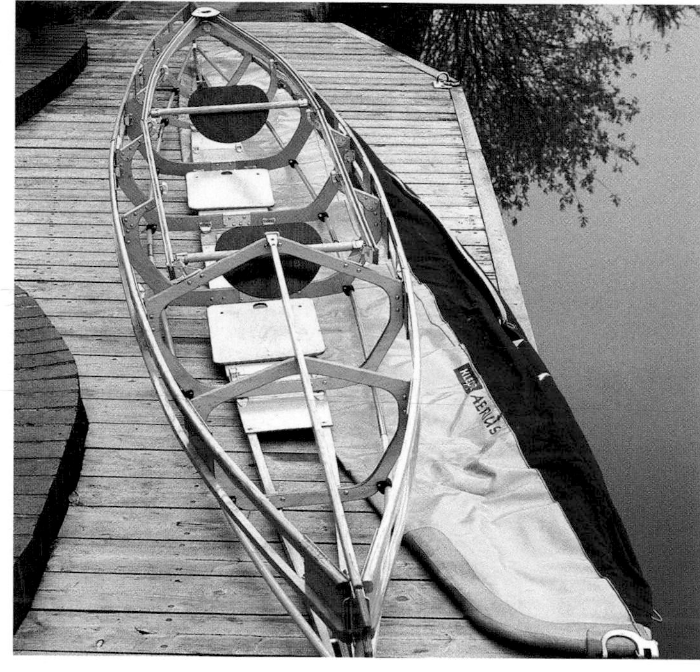

The Klepper folding kayak mimics the construction style of skin-on-frame boats but now uses modern materials.

Plastic Fantastic

During the latter half of the twentieth century, kayaking and canoeing received a dramatic boost from new technology. In the 1950s, the prevalent form of construction was still canvas over a wooden frame, and the paddles were made exclusively from wood. But, within 20 years, fibreglass (or glass-reinforced plastic) had totally revolutionized boat construction, and most boats were now made this way. For the first time it was possible to make more rounded shapes, and countless new designs soon flooded the paddling world.

In the 1980s, fibreglass and even more advanced composites, such as carbon fibre and Kevlar™, were dramatically overshadowed by plastic. The advent of plastic suddenly made it possible to mass-produce cheap and durable kayaks or canoes whose performance could almost rival the more expensive and fragile composite boats.

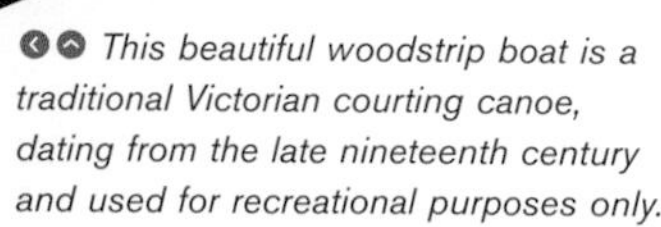

This beautiful woodstrip boat is a traditional Victorian courting canoe, dating from the late nineteenth century and used for recreational purposes only.

The Percy Blandford Kayak, or PBK, is an example of a wood and canvas boat from the 1950s. The construction method used is similar to the early Inuit kayaks.

Wooden battens line the floor of the PBK to protect the boat's fragile canvas skin when the paddler steps in.

The first fibreglass kayaks were not so different from their wood and canvas forebears. This 1960s example is more manoeuvrable because of its shorter length.

The next progression in general-purpose kayak design was to make the boats slightly wider behind the cockpit and higher in front, for better rough-water handling. This boat was used on extreme white water during the Descent of Everest Expedition in 1975.

For steep descents in heavy white water, boats became rounder, to give more control, and bigger in volume, with end grabs and foot rests.

Introducing the Kayak

The modern general-purpose kayak is so strong and versatile that even moderately experienced practitioners can tackle difficult feats. That is one reason why kayaking has recently become so popular, with many disciplines that provide all the thrills and spills of surfing.

Changing Shape and Form

Canoes might have remained largely unchanged while they were used primarily as a means of transport, but the design of kayaks for sport gradually deviated from their original look. Those used for recreation have become unrecognizable from the original Inuit style, which is now only retained by sea kayaks designed for open-sea use.

The kayak became a recreational and sporting boat in the twentieth century, and quickly adapted two forms. The flat water touring and racing kayak shape has derived from the rowing shell or skiff and, as the rowing boat became narrower and more rounded, so did the kayak. By the 1930s, the general-purpose and white water kayak had settled into a fairly widely accepted form, about 4m (13ft) long and 60cm (2ft) wide across the beam. The ultimate derivatives of these boat designs were seen in slalom and white water racing competitions, and for most of the late twentieth century they were the driving force behind the new look of the kayaks and decked canoes.

At about the same time, slalom racers realized that the boats performed much better if they were very low in volume, with thin pointed ends that could dip under the hanging poles, and slice better through the water to save time as they raced down the course. This development resulted in the invention of many of the techniques that have shaped the sport as it is today, and changed the way kayaks and decked canoes look forever.

The Influence of Plastic

The widespread introduction of mass-produced plastic boats in the 1980s brought further changes, both to the look of kayaks and the way in which they were used. Before then, boats belonged either to the high-performance competitive market and featured sleek, low-volume craft handmade from space-age composite materials, or they were recreational designs, typically more rounded, general-purpose boats made of plastic. Then, technological developments began to produce plastic boats that had many of the performance characteristics of the handmade models, combined with greater durability, and because they were cheaper to make, they were relatively inexpensive.

This change marked the end of slalom and river racing as the pinnacle to which every white water paddler aspired; both now became marginalized by the very different activities that the new plastic boats had made possible.

New Disciplines

The plastic revolution enabled even paddlers of intermediate ability to attempt white water descents that would have been impossible even for the most skilled paddler in the older, composite boats. This was partly because the new boats were more likely to bounce off rocks without mishap, and because they were shorter and more manoeuvrable.

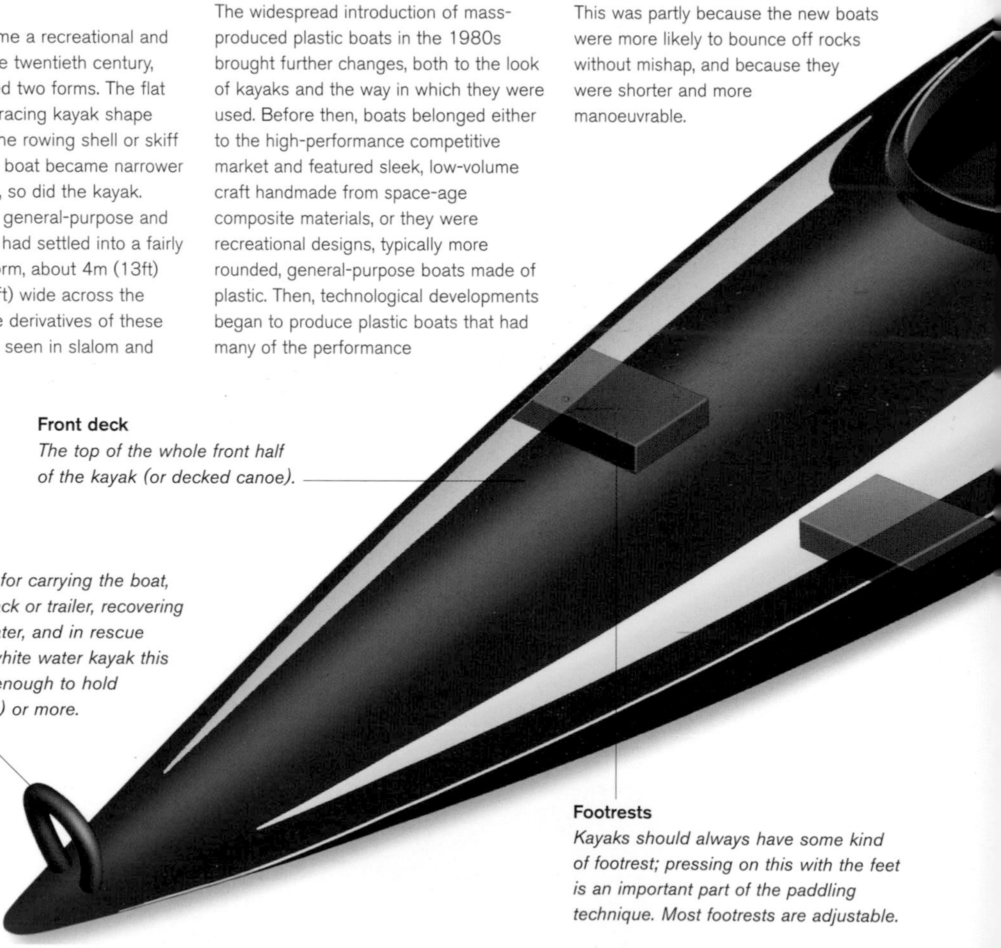

Front deck
The top of the whole front half of the kayak (or decked canoe).
Bow or end grab
This can be used for carrying the boat, tying it to a roof rack or trailer, recovering the boat in the water, and in rescue situations. On a white water kayak this would be strong enough to hold 1000kg (2200lbs) or more.
Footrests
Kayaks should always have some kind of footrest; pressing on this with the feet is an important part of the paddling technique. Most footrests are adjustable.

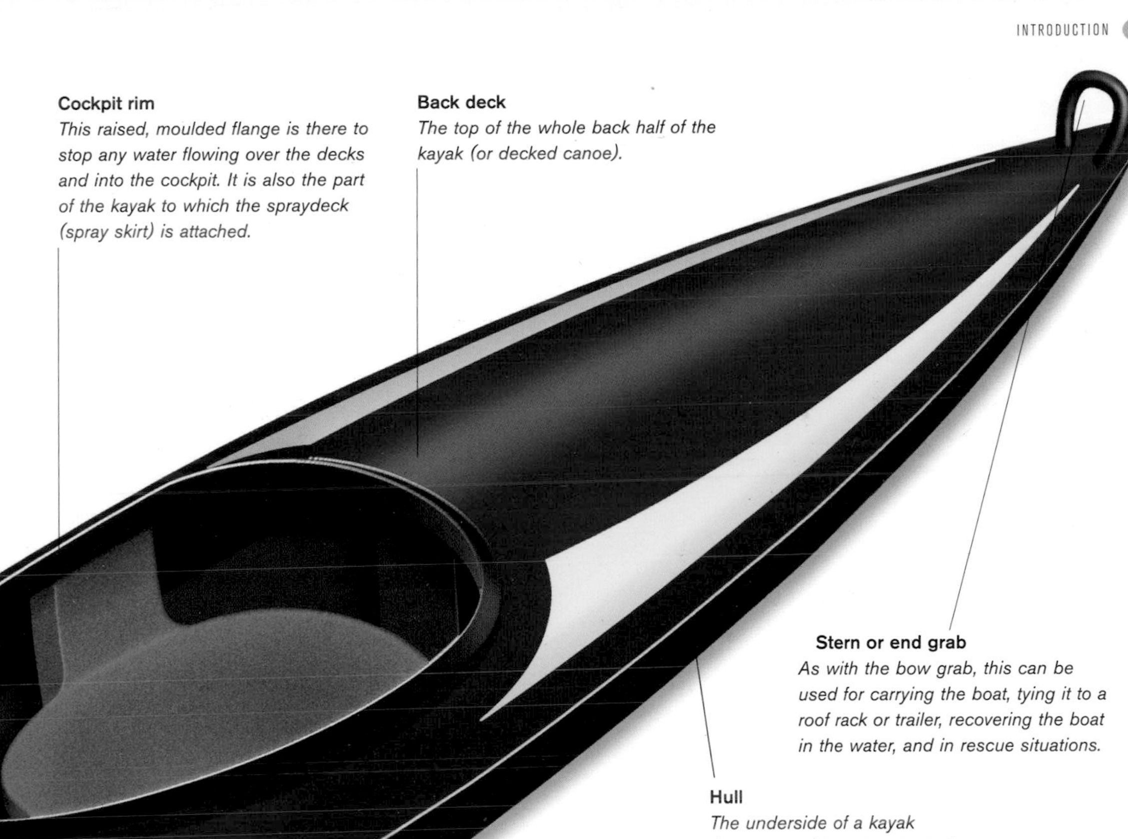

Cockpit rim
This raised, moulded flange is there to stop any water flowing over the decks and into the cockpit. It is also the part of the kayak to which the spraydeck (spray skirt) is attached.
Back deck
The top of the whole back half of the kayak (or decked canoe).
Stern or end grab
As with the bow grab, this can be used for carrying the boat, tying it to a roof rack or trailer, recovering the boat in the water, and in rescue situations.
Hull
The underside of a kayak (or any boat) is called the hull.
Rail or edge
Some boats are quite rounded, but many have sharp corners between the deck and side, and the side and hull. These are called rails or edges, and can be used to hydrodynamic effect by a skilled paddler.

Initially, short boats were frowned upon by the more conservative, traditional paddlers, but the designers kept creating even shorter models. The stage has now been reached whereby the boats cannot get any shorter because the paddlers' feet are so close to the end of the boat. This development, more than any other, has altered white water paddling for ever. It has also meant that many of the skills and strokes practised today are unique to the newer boats now in common use.

Plastic boats made descents of extreme white water possible for the first time, and enabled white water boaters to perform demanding, high-energy manoeuvres that would previously have smashed a lightweight competition boat. In short, plastic led to the sport of freestyle kayaking, where paddlers perform acrobatic tricks on white water and create complex routines to be judged on style and technical ability.

Meanwhile, the flat water touring and competition scene continued largely unaffected by the plastic revolution. The competitive side is best seen at the Olympics, and features very long, narrow and unstable sprint boats. They, and other similar boats, can also be used for fast inland touring. Touring boats with better rough water handling have been designed for less sheltered conditions and coastal use, while the Inuit-style sea kayak is extremely popular for more demanding estuary and ocean paddling.

Paddling on the sea taught kayakers how to handle their craft in surf and waves, which in turn led to the popular sport of kayak surfing. A number of kayak styles can be used to ride waves like surfers do, and to perform tricks and manoeuvres. Competitions for kayak surfing judge paddlers on the style and quality of their rides, as with freestyle kayaking.

Introducing the Canoe

Many canoes today look remarkably similar to their traditional Native American ancestors. Some, such as those used for racing, slalom and freestyle, look entirely different. All have benefited from the advances in materials technology that changed kayaking forever, but there are still many canoe paddlers who prefer to adhere to tradition.

The canoe remained largely unchanged in shape and concept while it was used as a means of transport. Apart from the Polynesian canoes and outrigger boats that were used for fishing and inter-island sailing, the prevalent form has always been the open boat with an upswept bow and stern associated with the North American hunters and trappers. Once the canoe became a recreational and sporting boat in the twentieth century, new developments began.

Open Canoes

Many of today's open canoes look much like the traditional models. Materials and construction techniques may have altered, but in form and function they remain virtually unchanged. While these boats are unsuitable for open sea touring, there is and always will be a tradition of using open boats for inland touring. There are many traditionalists who prefer to paddle an open canoe, using air bags or buoyancy tanks to stop the boat sinking in heavy water. For the family and recreational user, the relatively low purchase price and durability of the open canoe make it an extremely practical choice of boat for general-purpose use.

Decked Canoes

Decking in the top part of the boat is a logical move to keep the paddler dry in rough water conditions. Decked boats were initially designed for performance and the more extreme disciplines.

Decked boats were best seen in action in slalom and white water racing competitions, and for most of the latter part of the twentieth century the needs of these disciplines were the driving force behind much of the commercial development in canoes. The single-seater competition canoe, known as the C1, became, for all intents and purposes, like a kayak in design, except for the kneeling position and the smaller cockpit. The two-seater competition canoe, or C2, had cockpits at either end, although competitive racing meant that the cockpits were moved as close to the centre of the boat as possible, to provide sharper manoeuvrability.

At about the same time, slalom racers realized – as with kayaks – that the boats performed much better if they were less buoyant (very low in volume), with thin, pointed ends that could pass underneath the vertical hanging poles of the slalom course, and carve a quicker passage through the water. The move towards low-volume boats led, in turn, to the development of many of the handling techniques seen in the sport today.

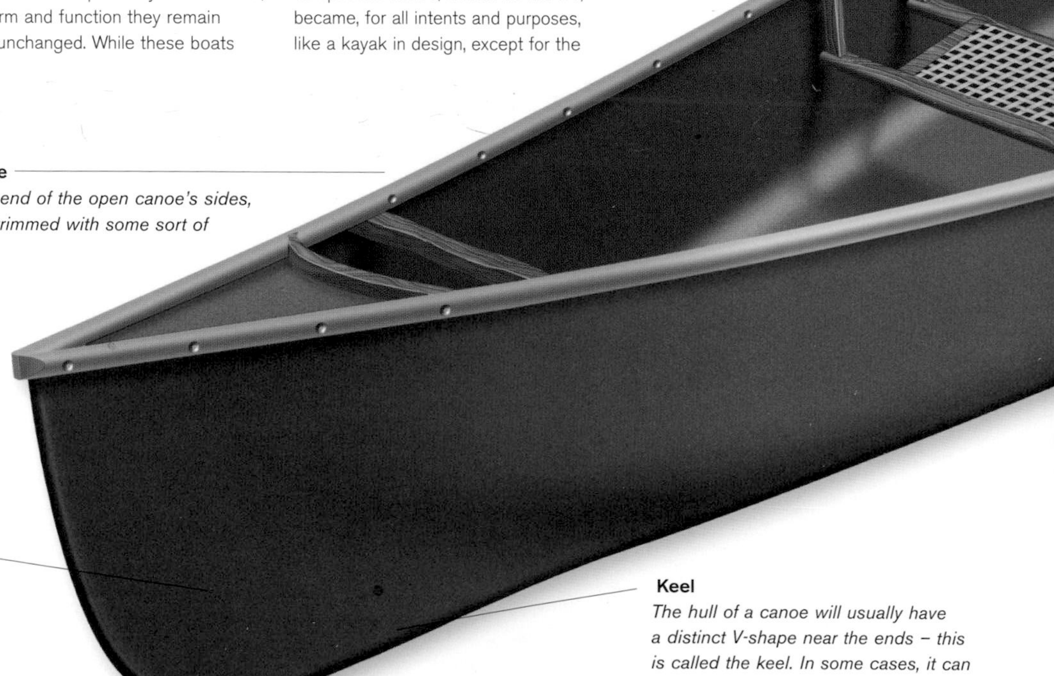

Gunwale
The top end of the open canoe's sides, usually trimmed with some sort of flange.

Bow or prow
The front end of a canoe.

Keel
The hull of a canoe will usually have a distinct V-shape near the ends – this is called the keel. In some cases, it can extend throughout the length of the boat.

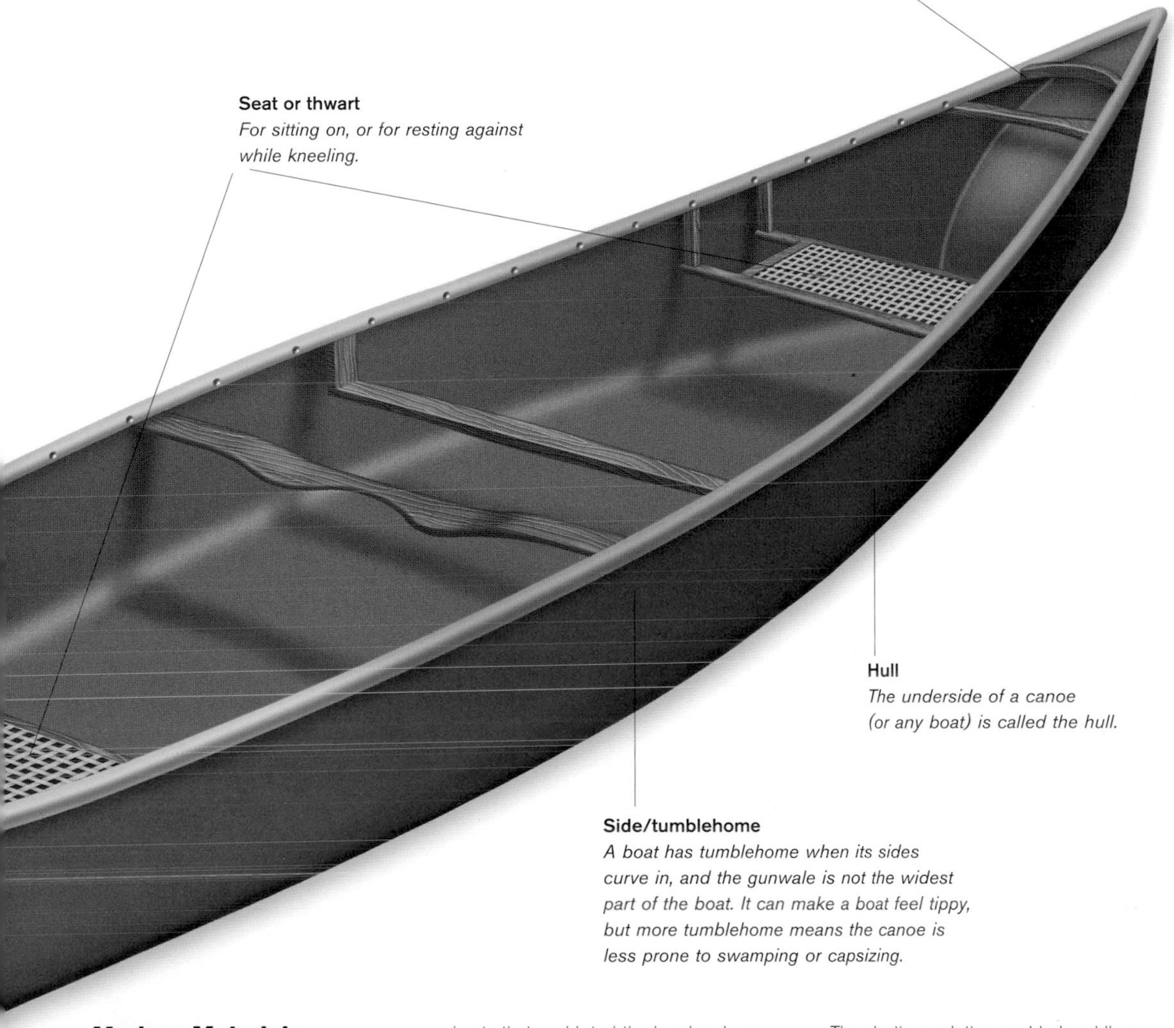

Stern
The back end of a canoe.

Seat or thwart
For sitting on, or for resting against while kneeling.

Hull
The underside of a canoe (or any boat) is called the hull.

Side/tumblehome
A boat has tumblehome when its sides curve in, and the gunwale is not the widest part of the boat. It can make a boat feel tippy, but more tumblehome means the canoe is less prone to swamping or capsizing.

Modern Materials

The arrival of plastic boats in the 1980s had huge repercussions on the sport. Before then the canoe world had two very distinct groups. At the top end of the scale were the expensive low-volume decked boats used by the high-performance competitive scene, which were handmade from the latest materials. Meanwhile, the recreational scene was still dominated by general-purpose open boats made of fibreglass or wood. By the 1970s, technological developments led to plastic boats that could rival the handmade ones; they were tougher and less expensive, and allowed white water paddlers to have bigger aspirations than slalom and river racing. The plastic boats of the 1980s gave an extra edge to the competitive world of canoeing, changing it completely.

The new plastic canoes, like the new kayaks, were becoming so manoeuvrable they could perform increasingly aggressive moves. This led to the sport of freestyle canoeing, where paddlers take turns to perform elaborate tricks on white water.

The plastic revolution enabled paddlers of intermediate ability to attempt descents (not always safely) that would have been beyond even skilled boaters in the older, composite boats. The new boats were tough and could withstand knocks against rocks, and they were highly manoeuvrable. While there were dramatic developments in white water canoeing, flat water touring, slalom and competitions continued largely unaffected. The Olympic Games is still the focus for long, narrow and unstable sprint canoes.

Different Types of Canoes and Kayaks

While everyone has a mental picture of what is meant by them, the words "canoe" and "kayak" encompass such a wide spectrum of designs that it can be difficult to know where to start. Canoes are in a sense easier, since although there are many types, the more common ones you are likely to come across as a beginner all look much the same, however many subtle differences they may harbour. Kayaks, on the other hand, are now commonly found in such a bewildering variety of shapes and sizes that the beginner will almost certainly need advice from someone experienced before getting involved.

Types of Canoes

Open canoes fall into two broad categories – those used for flatwater and those for whitewater. The whitewater ones can be identified by their airbags and complex internal fittings, and are best avoided by beginners if only because they are so difficult to paddle in a straight line! Almost any other open boat is suitable for beginners, as long as it has a fairly flat bottom in the middle part of the hull. Some of the more rounded designs can be a bit wobbly!

Canoes are available in various lengths and with a variety of seating positions, some intended for solo use, some double or more. Most are versatile and can be paddled solo even if large enough to accommodate a small family and picnic. You should be aware that a large boat can be too heavy to carry unaided.

There are also decked canoes, which are for all intents and purposes the same as kayaks, but paddled in a kneeling position with a canoe blade.

Types of Kayaks

Kayaks come in a wider variety of designs. A surprising number of them are suitable for beginners, but you might need to seek expert advice before investing in one.

Sit-on Kayaks are eminently suitable for beginners. These plastic or foam kayaks do not enclose your legs, and are blissfully free of unnecessary encumbrances. These surprisingly versatile boats are great fun, stable, and cannot fill up with water or sink. The only disadvantage is that if you become more advanced you may find you want to be better attached to the boat than is easily achievable with a sit-on-top. Solo and double versions are available. Don't mistake a wave-ski for a sit-on kayak – they look similar but wave-skis are made for advanced paddlers to use in the surf.

General Purpose Kayaks are usually about 3m (10ft) long and 60cm (2ft) wide, and made of plastic. These kayaks have a deck enclosing your legs and a cockpit opening which can be sealed with a spraydeck. They are usually fairly stable and quite easy to paddle in a straight line, but you need to be confident about getting out if you capsize.

Touring Kayaks are usually about 4m (13ft) long, sometimes more. They are very stable and very easy to paddle in a straight line. In fact they can be slow to turn for a beginner, unless fitted with a rudder. They are closed deck boats, but they usually have such a big cockpit that it isn't at all hard to get out. They can be made from plastic or glassfibre-type composite materials, and are easily identified by their high, ship-like bow and stern.

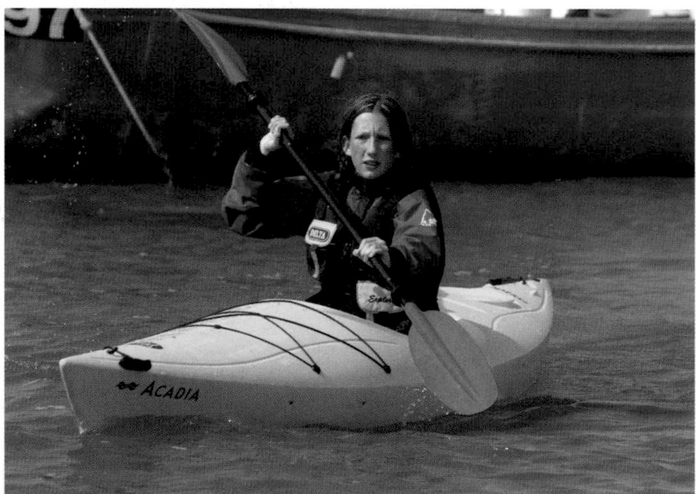

▲ A specialist closed cockpit touring kayak with shockcord on the deck for maps or accessories.

◄ A closed cockpit general purpose kayak, suitable for any kind of paddling.

Sea Kayaks are normally over 4.5m (15ft) long. They are similar to touring boats but usually have distinctive upswept bow and stern. They are often characterized by rope decklines and other specialist fittings such as hatches and compass mountings. Often made of plastic but more commonly glassfibre, these boats are suitable for beginners but are specially designed for sea trips and aren't terribly versatile. They are less stable and harder to steer than most other types of boat.

Racing/Fast Touring Kayaks are usually 4.5m (15ft) long, low and narrow, and wider behind the cockpit than in front. They look appealing to beginners because of their rakish lines and big cockpits, but they are terribly wobbly and not a suitable first boat at all. Whitewater kayaks can be identified by their short length (under 3m/10ft) and rounded ends. Made from plastic, they are actually fine for beginners to use, but they are quite expensive and have a lot of features that are only intended for use on rapids. They are very stable, and very easy to turn. Perhaps they are a little too difficult to paddle straight for some people, but many find it acceptable. If you intend to take up whitewater paddling at some point, you could do worse than start with a boat like this.

A sit-on kayak has the advantage that the paddler's legs are not inside the boat, and takes less getting used to.

A two-person, open cockpit kayak. A good compromise between the closed cockpit boat and the sit-on – the paddlers sit inside the boat and stay fairly dry, but their legs are not really under the deck, so it's much easier to get in and out.

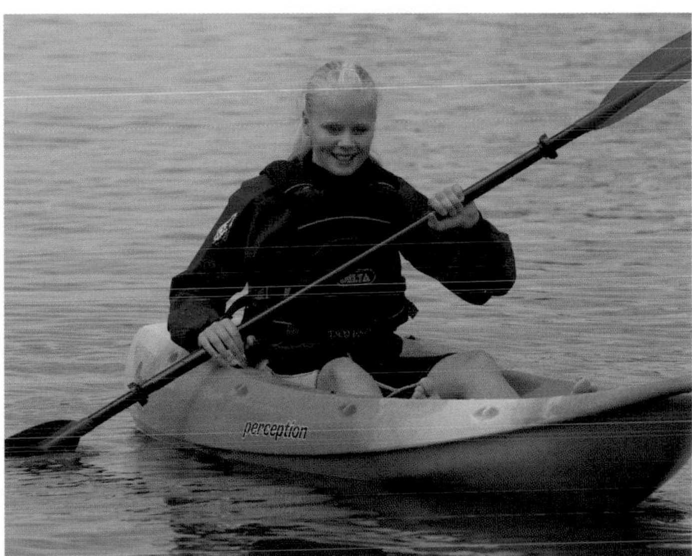

Whitewater Playboats are very short (sub-2.5m or 8ft) and have a flat bottom and thin ends. They are very stable but very difficult for a beginner to paddle in a straight line. Sometimes it is barely possible to keep both ends afloat at the same time. They often have aggressive internal fittings that make it hard to get in and out, so are best avoided by beginners.

Slalom Kayaks are made from glassfibre and are 4m (13ft) long. They are very pointy at the ends and have a fairly rounded hull. They are not unsuitable for beginners as long as they aren't too low in volume, but they are hard to paddle straight. They are fairly stable though, and can be picked up very cheaply second-hand.

GETTING STARTED

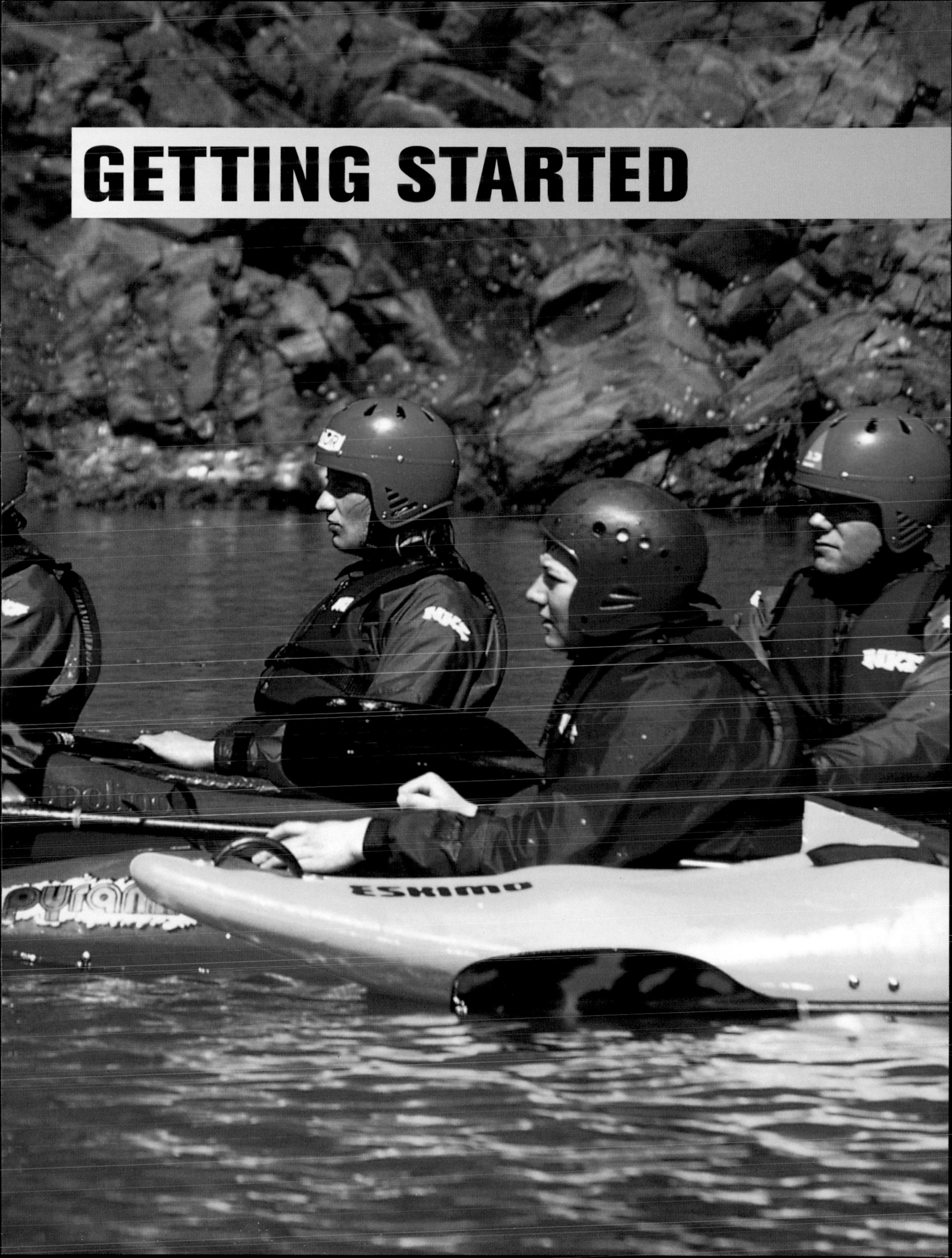

GOING PADDLING FOR THE FIRST TIME

There are a wide variety of paddle sports, ranging from the placid to the frankly insane, and it pays to be sure that you know what you are getting into. Most people take the gentle approach, and learn to paddle on completely safe, flat, sheltered water. Even so, many kayaks and canoes seem initially unstable, and for most people that is exactly what distinguishes these craft from more solid dinghies and rowing boats.

The possibility of being capsized means that you have to take certain precautions. Being able to swim at least 50m (170ft) in clothing is a prerequisite, and wearing a buoyancy aid (personal flotation device, or PFD) is important, particularly when you start because you might fall into the water quite often. What is more often overlooked is the need to think through what will happen if you do end up in the water. Will the boat float? Will you be able to get ashore quickly? Is there land close by?

These considerations are covered in this chapter. The important point when starting out is to think about your personal safety; do not just jump into a boat and paddle off. Canoeing and kayaking are not dangerous, but a cavalier approach most certainly is.

Two kayakers in traditional Inuit-style boats cruising up a beautiful estuary.

Paddlers getting organized in plastic general-purpose boats.

Where and When to Paddle

Boating is great fun, but it pays to be careful. Stick to the elementary rules and always put safety first. A few minutes' careful checking before you get into the water is all that is required.

Suitable Waters

Until you have achieved the level of self-sufficiency that sets a kayaker or canoeist apart from someone just "having a go", it is best to seek out safe, predictable environments to paddle in, where there is help at hand if required.

You should learn to paddle on still water, although this is often surprisingly hard to find. Non-tidal rivers and lakes in calm weather, or reservoirs where public access to the water is allowed, would be suitable, but make sure there is good bank access in case you have to swim ashore. Beaches are generally safe for beginners as long as the waves are less than 2m (6½ft) and the wind is not blowing offshore. Find out about the character of the stretch of beach you plan to use in advance, and make sure there are no strong currents you cannot see.

The points to consider on a beach are wave size, wind and water currents.

Sheltered inland waterways such as this river are ideal for safe paddling.

For novices in search of trouble-free water, inland lakes are best of all.

Where Not to Paddle

There are a number of situations that are unsuitable for paddling. Some situations can present difficulties, while others are dangerous. It pays to know what to avoid.

Do not paddle where the wind or current can carry you away faster than you can paddle or swim. In fact, avoid fast currents when learning; it is far easier to learn if the conditions are in your favour.

Do not paddle where it might be difficult to get out of the water. Remember that you might be cold and tired after capsizing. Avoid any obstacle that might present a problem, such as steep banks, deep mud and slippery rocks, which can be a nightmare to the tired paddler with a boat full of water.

If there is a current, avoid paddling where there are rocks, trees, pontoons or obstructions in the water. A barely visible current can be enough to pin a boat or a person against the upstream side of an obstruction, and this is a common cause of paddling accidents.

Always stay away from weirs. Do not approach them either from above or below. Not all weirs are dangerous, but it takes experience to be able to tell a friendly weir from a dangerous one, and even friendly weirs have minor hazards. The only safe policy is to give them a wide berth unless you are an experienced and confident white water paddler who chooses to accept the risk. To beginners, weirs represent a genuine threat to safety and should be avoided at all costs.

Beware of water flowing beneath low bridges, such as this. Although the water here is fairly slow-moving, it could easily pull you along with it. If your boat were to jam under the low bridge, you could find yourself in trouble very quickly.

Do not paddle on fast-flowing water until you have learned a range of skills.

Weirs can be extremely dangerous for paddlers, and it is always advisable to stay away from them.

Serious Hazards

Some situations can and do prove fatal. It is imperative that you are aware of the dangers involved with any of the following.

River Levels

Be aware that river levels can rise and fall very suddenly. This might only affect your access to or exit from a river, but it could turn a friendly stream into a lethal one.

Rivers rise because of the amount of rainfall or because of snow melt. Many mountain rivers rise very dramatically in the afternoon because the sun melts the snow or ice, and the water produced reaches the river a few hours later.

The mud banks and reeds here would make it very difficult to get out of the river with your boat.

Compare these two pictures, taken on the same day. The water level has risen 1m (3½ft) and turned a meandering stream into a potentially lethal torrent after several hours of rain.

Beware when paddling upstream of any obstruction in the river, especially if the water can flow through or under it, as in the case of this log-jam. The current could very easily force you into or under such an obstruction.

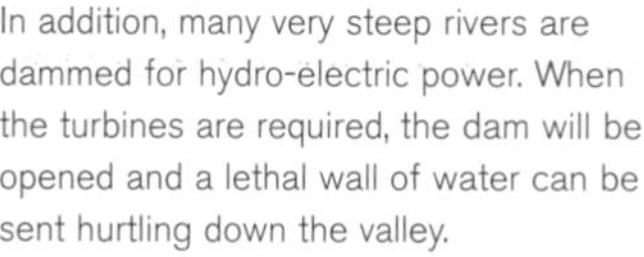

In addition, many very steep rivers are dammed for hydro-electric power. When the turbines are required, the dam will be opened and a lethal wall of water can be sent hurtling down the valley.

Strainers and Siphons

These are usually found on white water rivers, but they can occur anywhere the water is flowing at a significant speed.

A barrier through which water flows, such as a fallen tree or log jam is called a strainer because it lets water pass through but will catch anything solid. These are very dangerous. Do not risk being swept into the upstream side of one.

Even more dangerous is the siphon, where water disappears underground. Get too close and you will be sucked down too, and possibly jammed stuck.

Preparing to Paddle

When first learning to paddle, it is best to practise in a familiar area, within sight of a reliable launching and landing place, instead of attempting any kind of journey. As you build up your experience, and become more familiar with the boat and the basic manoeuvring techniques, you will be able to go further afield and use your boat to explore.

Once you have become hooked on boating, it is very easy to become complacent and to imagine that you are more experienced and more capable than you really are. Beware of asking too much of yourself too soon. Remember your own limitations and, just as importantly, those of the other members of your group. A failure to do this can seriously compromise your safety, and no amount of fun will justify this risk.

Are You Up To It?

It is vital that you have a realistic idea of the kind of distance you can paddle, and that you know your own limitations in terms of ability, fitness and strength: some people are surprised at how quickly they become tired in a boat out on the water. Remember, too, that you could get hot, cold, tired, hungry or dehydrated according to the weather conditions. While this might not be any different from when going for a long walk, if any of these conditions affect you severely while you are on or near the water, the consequences can be far more serious. Consider this before you set out, and make sure that you are properly equipped.

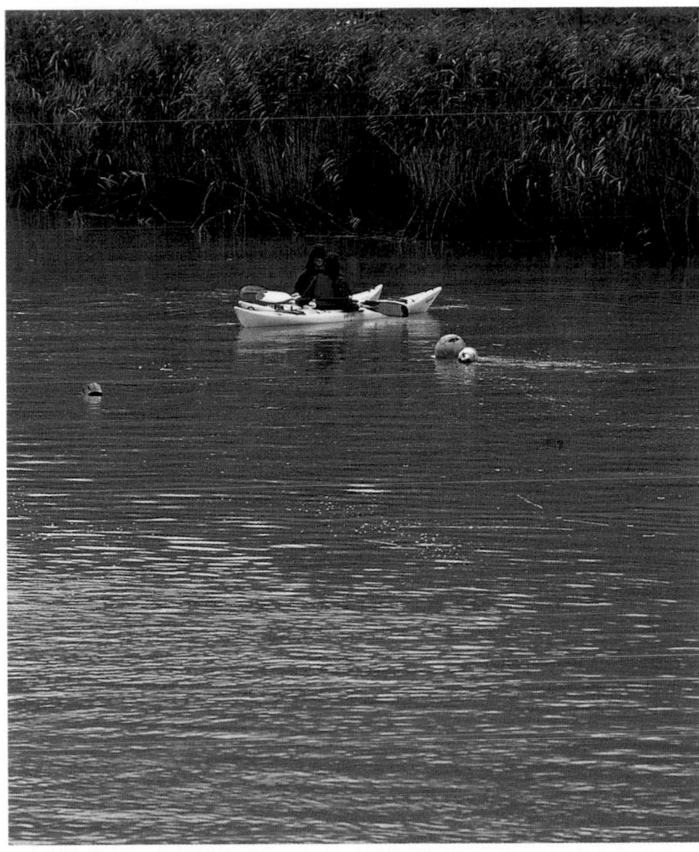

Paddlers will often "raft up" to give themselves a rest if anyone in the group is feeling tired.

CHECKLIST

If the answer to any of the following questions is "No", reassess your plan before you set out on the water.

- Is everyone in the group capable of looking after themselves? If not, will some be able to look after the others?
- Do you have all the appropriate equipment for today's trip?
- Does everyone know how many hours they will paddle for?
- Are you sure that you can get to where you intend to go in that time?
- Does someone on land know where the group is going and what time they are expected to finish?

Advance Planning

It always pays to be prepared for likely eventualities. Make it a key part of your preparation routine to plan the route of your journey, using an up-to-date Ordnance Survey 1:50,000 map. If your group can all do this together, so much the better. Listen to a detailed weather report for the area on the day of your trip and consider how the weather is likely to affect the water conditions. If you know what to expect, you will be able to make an informed choice to continue with the trip, to resort to the contingency plan or to put the whole thing off for another day in order to avoid anything too severe that might cause you problems. Check that you have the right type of clothing and equipment for the conditions, and enough food and drinking water to see you through to the end of your trip. Finally, consider the needs of the weakest member(s) of the group and adapt your preparation plan accordingly, allowing more time for the journey and more provisions as necessary. Your plan must take account of all levels of expertise if everyone is to have an enjoyable time.

Exposure to the Elements

Whether you are boating on an inland stream or out at sea, you are generally more exposed to the elements than when you are on land. It is necessary to take precautions since the effects of heat and cold, and sudden changes of wind direction, can strike very suddenly.

Sun

When you are out on the water, the effects of the sun are greater than normal, and ultimately these may dictate how long you can stay out. It is quite possible to get severe sunburn in as little as 30 minutes on the water on a day when you could sunbathe on the shore for much longer. It is extremely important that you always take with you an adequate sunscreen for your face, neck, arms and legs. If you are not wearing a helmet, protect your head and the back of your neck with a sunhat or baseball cap to minimize the risk of sunstroke.

Wind

The effects of wind are also much more pronounced when you are on the water. A light breeze ashore, which necessitates no more than a thin summer shirt, might cause serious wind chill when you are afloat. As a general guide, there are few days when you will not need a windproof top plus at least one thermal layer, even when the sun is out and the weather is hot. If you are wet after a swim, these potential problems will all be magnified.

Always take with you a selection of clothes that allow you to adjust your level of insulation during the course of the trip.

Never go paddling during a gale. High winds make it almost impossible to control a kayak or canoe, and you will struggle to hang on to your paddle. In addition, the water will become rough and unpredictable. You won't be able to make forward progress against anything more than a stiff breeze but, bizarrely, it is a following wind or a crosswind that make the boat hardest to control. Accept that strong winds and paddling just don't mix, unless you are equipped to sail your boat.

Rain

It can be very pleasant to paddle in the rain if you are sensibly dressed. On the other hand, it can be a miserable experience if you aren't. Being cold and wet at the same time is uncomfortable and it can become a real problem if the temperature is low. If rain is likely, make sure you pack a waterproof garment. A woollen hat or a hood on your jacket or cagoule can make a huge difference to how you feel. Reducing the heat loss from your head is an effective remedy when you are cold, and in the rain, headgear will stop water constantly running down your face, which can become very uncomfortable.

Lightning

Although it is a lot more rare than a situation involving strong currents or a sudden change in the weather, lightning is one of the most dangerous weather phenomena for paddlers. On the land you are unlikely to be struck by lightning. On open water, it is a different matter. Anything sticking up out of the water is in danger, and that means you. You also have a long pole (your paddle) in your hands to add to the effect. On land, the people most likely to be struck by lightning are golfers because they stand in the middle of open spaces holding golf clubs that serve as

Paddlers out at sea are exposed to sun, wind chill and salt spray.

conductive objects. As a boater, you are taking the lightning attractor concept several stages further because lightning is more likely to strike a solitary object on water than on land. If the weather report suggests storms, don't go out at all; if a storm blows up while you are on the water, get ashore as quickly as possible.

Extreme Hot and Cold

Luckily, you are unlikely to experience extreme heat and cold in the same location. However, if you go paddling in an extreme climate, your usual paddling clothing may not be appropriate, and you will need to consider other safety issues.

In hot climates, apart from the dangers of sunburn and sunstroke, there is a real danger of dehydration and heat stroke. The most important thing is to keep drinking water. If you feel thirsty, you are already dehydrated. If you cannot quench your thirst, or have a limited water supply, you need to get into the shade and cool down. One of the problems with very hot, tropical environments is the humidity. The air is so saturated that the process of sweating does not cool you down, although your body doesn't realize and carries on sweating. This is why you get dehydrated even though you may be soaking wet the whole time.

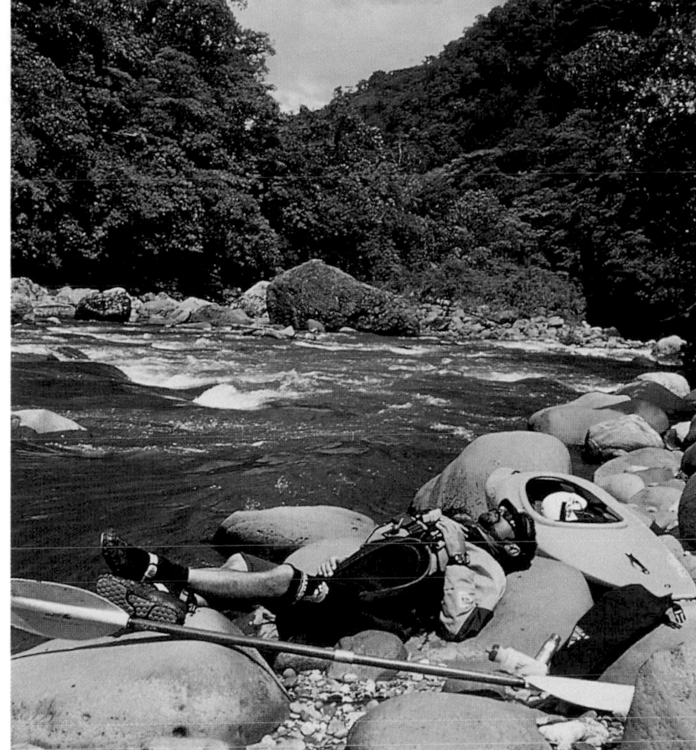

Taking a rest in the hot midday sunshine. This paddler would be at risk without his drinking water, sunscreen and protective hat.

Make sure you are equipped for all weather conditions before you set out.

In very cold air or water, the key is to dress to be both warm and dry. If you get soaked in a freezing environment you only have a few minutes to get warm and dry before you start to suffer from hypothermia. For practical reasons, then, a dry suit is needed for severely cold conditions. This will ensure that you don't get wet from immersion. Wear gloves or mitts on your hands: they will prevent the pain of frozen fingers.

Managing Body Temperature

By far the best way to control your body temperature is to wear good quality thermal base layers, which will work with your body's inherent control mechanism. A versatile cagoule with adjustable seals will allow you to adjust your temperature by opening and closing the neck or rolling up the sleeves. If you wear conventional manmade fabrics, you will find yourself endlessly putting on extra clothes and taking them off as your body heats and cools down too rapidly.

Basic Safety and Rescue

It might be tempting to think that you are quite experienced, and can cope with any potential danger, but the rule is, always, "Beginners beware!" Make sure you and your group are up to the challenge.

Safety in Numbers

When out on the water, there should always be at least three people in the group. In the event of an accident or a medical emergency, one person can stay with the victim and the other can go for help. It is even better if there are four or five people, so that no one has to deal with emergencies alone, but if there are too many in the group then other logistical problems arise, even when things are going smoothly. Experienced paddlers may choose to ignore this basic safety rule, but they only do so when they feel totally confident about taking risks. Beginners should always stick to the rule.

Assessing your Group

You must be sure that the group is capable of taking care of itself as a unit, and can sort out any problems as they arise. Everyone should be able to swim 50m (170ft) in their clothing, and flotation aids should always be worn when afloat. But what if a boat has filled with water? Will the group be able to empty it and get the paddler back in? Or tow the victim back to shore? And what if the location turns out to be trickier than imagined, or the distance greater? Will the group have the skills required to get a tired paddler back to safety if they cannot paddle alone?

These are crucial questions. If the answers to any of them are "No", then you should restrict your paddling to safe locations, such as a beach or small lake, where everyone could make it ashore, and there are no significant safety threats.

CHECKLIST

Some of the following safety gear is optional but what you choose to carry should be dictated by conditions. If in doubt, or if the conditions are variable, take it anyway.

- Bivvy bag
- Drinking water and a hot drink (optional)
- First aid kit
- Repair kit
- Diver's knife or folding saw
- Spare paddle (optional)
- Throw line (optional)
- 1:50,000 map
- Torch
- Whistle
- Tow line
- Flares if at sea or on a very large lake (optional)

The husky tow, in which one paddler is pulled by two, is used for long distances.

Assisted tow. A tired paddler is helped and towed by her companions.

Rescue Procedures

Although you may be unfamiliar with paddling a canoe or kayak, let alone rescuing one, it is a good idea to know what to expect if you find yourself in need of a tow because of tiredness or injury, or if you are swimming in the water after a capsize. If you are already an accomplished paddler, these techniques can be used to help a fellow boater in the event of a mishap.

What to do in the event of a capsize is covered in detail at the beginning of the chapters on kayaking and canoeing skills. If you are unable to roll your boat, your priority is to get out. Once out, you can be carried back to shore on the front or back of another paddler's boat, or you can be helped back into your own boat while it is still afloat, using a X-rescue or, for a larger boat, a H-rescue. If you need a pull because of tiredness or injury, your fellow paddlers can use a husky tow or an assisted tow to help you back to shore.

Practising basic rescue skills is an important part of becoming a competent paddler. If everyone in your group is familiar with the rescue skills shown opposite, the group will be self-sufficient, as well as safer and more confident.

X-rescue

1 Drag the boat across the rescuer's deck, and rock it to and fro to empty it of water. Constantly reassure the victim, who may be in shock.

2 Put the empty boat back in the water, the right way up and alongside, and with the stern next to, the rescuer's bow. Place both paddles across the decks.

3 The victim can lift his legs up out of the water and over the paddles, keeping an equal amount of body weight on each boat. Keep reassuring the victim.

4 The rescuer holds the victim's boat to stop the two boats floating apart. The victim shuffles forward until he is able to put his feet into his boat.

5 Shifting the weight across, the victim is now entirely back on his own boat, and is ready to climb back in. The rescuer can hold his boat steady as he does this.

6 With the rescued paddler now securely back in his boat, he can take his paddle and push off from the rescuer's boat to continue the trip.

Alternative Rescue Techniques

One paddler tows the empty boat, while another paddler carries the tired swimmer on the back of their boat.

Heavier larger boats can be difficult to empty using the X-rescue. Some paddlers use a H-rescue, which involves two boats, as shown here.

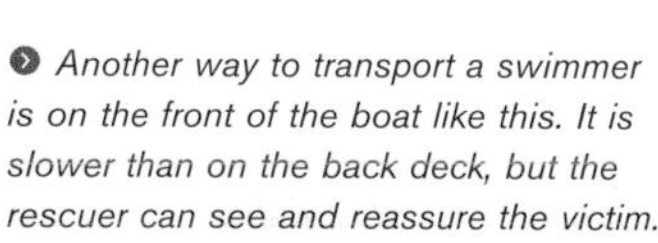

Another way to transport a swimmer is on the front of the boat like this. It is slower than on the back deck, but the rescuer can see and reassure the victim.

EQUIPMENT AND PREPARATION

From a sport that, in the 1980s, had little in the way of specialized equipment, kayaking and canoeing have certainly come a long way. The clothing and safety equipment, and the boats and paddles, are now quite sophisticated and high-tech. This is thoroughly appropriate because sport on water is physically quite demanding.

When you first start boating, you will not need much in the way of specialist gear. If you only intend to splash about on flat water near to land, and never go far or encounter difficult conditions, the bare minimum may be perfectly adequate. If, on the other hand, you decide to progress, and try more demanding water conditions, you will find that there is an ever-increasing array of equipment that you must consider.

Sea kayakers wearing comprehensive paddling gear and in well-equipped boats.

A kayaker stretching in preparation for a session out on the water.

Kayaks

A huge range of kayaks are now available, and it is important that you check the following features. When buying a kayak, talk to the sales staff: ask the right questions, based on the following criteria, and make sure you are happy with the answers. If you are unable to find out what you want to know, you could contact kayak manufacturers for more information about their products.

• A kayak must have sufficient buoyancy to float when full of water, and provide you with something to hold on to if you are swimming alongside after capsizing. The buoyancy should be distributed so that the kayak floats level when swamped.

• It must have a seat, and a footrest to brace against, otherwise you will not be able to paddle it properly.

• Not advisable the first time out because it makes entry and exit more difficult, but beneficial thereafter, is padding either side of the hips. Without this, your body movements will not be transmitted to the boat and the boat's movements will not be felt by you. Much of your body's energy is also delivered to the boat by your knees, so it is particularly important that the knees are held firmly in position. This is usually achieved by some sort of built-in grips or mouldings to hold the legs in place under the deck. Without these, the boat will not respond well to you or you to it.

This touring kayak is an all-round boat and a good first time buy.

This boat has been fitted out to a high standard with hard foam padding to hug the hips and legs, and make the paddler an integral part of the kayak.

Adjusting the backrest. This kayak has a modern fit system that allows you to fine-tune your position while you are seated in the boat.

TIPS

• The basics for going paddling are a kayak – which can be used with a spraydeck – or canoe, flotation aid, paddle, suitable clothing, helmet and safety and rescue equipment.

• Try out as many different pieces of equipment as you can before deciding which is for you.

• Before buying any equipment, make sure that you know exactly what you are going to do on the water. Only when you know how you want your equipment to perform can you make informed choices.

• All kayaks, except those used for competition or the more specialist disciplines, need to have end grabs, which give you something to hold on to if you need to tow the boat, or a capsized paddler in the water, to the shore.

• Be confident that you can get out of the kayak easily before you agree to use it on the water. Your paddling will not be very good if you are constantly worried that you will not be able to free yourself if the boat capsizes.

Spraydecks

A spraydeck (spray skirt) fits around your waist and over the cockpit to stop water getting into the boat. Spraydecks are not generally needed on flat water, where the water is calm, with little or no splashing.

Nylon spraydecks are commonly used for teaching beginners, but these can let in water because they are only really designed to be splash-proof. Neoprene ones are much drier and warmer, but they are more expensive and more difficult to fit and detach. You may not use a spraydeck at first, but if you do it is important that you can attach and remove it easily, without help. This can take quite a bit of practice.

Fitting a Spraydeck

Whichever type of spraydeck you use, you should be wearing it around your waist before you get in the kayak. Once you are sitting comfortably, and have made sure that you are not sitting on any part of the spraydeck, reach back with both hands and put the shock cord, or other attachment, under the cockpit rim at the back. Now feed the hands outwards, keeping some tension on the spraydeck, until you can pull forwards with both hands and fit the spraydeck over the front of the cockpit. Make sure that the release strap is outside and not trapped within. Familiarize yourself with where it is: you will need to find it quickly if you capsize.

To release the spraydeck, take the release strap in your hand and pull firmly upwards. It is usually better to pull a little forwards at the same time, rather than back. Once the spraydeck has been released from the front of the cockpit, run your hands under it right the way round to make sure it is totally free. It is annoying to start getting out of the boat and then come to an abrupt halt as the spraydeck pulls tight.

As a beginner you need a spraydeck that is easy to put on and release. It may not be very waterproof compared to other models on the market, but it will keep the kayak from filling up, and this is as much as you will need on flat water.

CHECKLIST

• Are you confident about the idea of wearing a spraydeck (spray skirt)? If not, don't agree to use one.
• Is the spraydeck the correct size for the boat? They do vary, so ask someone experienced to check.
• Is the spraydeck adjustable at the waist? If so, make it tight enough to hold up around the chest but without being uncomfortable.
• Is the release handle securely sewn on to the spraydeck? Never put one on a boat without checking this.
• Can you find the release handle with your eyes shut while sitting in the boat with the spraydeck fitted? If not, you are unlikely to be able to do it underwater. Practise until you know exactly where it is.

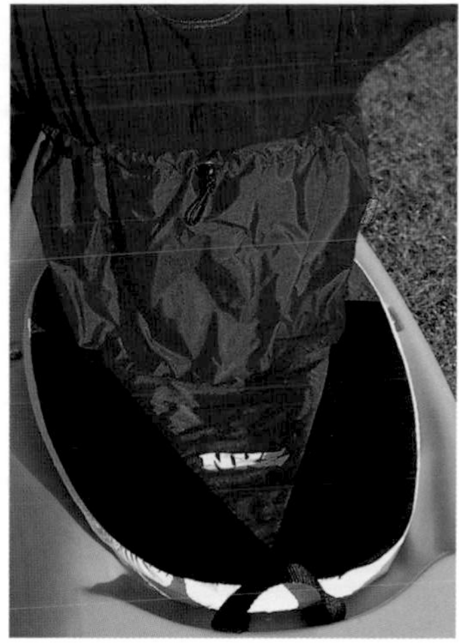

A nylon spraydeck (skirt) that might be used by a beginner on flat water.

Fitting your Spraydeck

1 Get into the kayak wearing the spraydeck (skirt). Fit the spraydeck under the cockpit rim at the back of the boat.

2 Feed the hands forward, keeping the spraydeck under tension so that it stays hooked under at the back.

3 Hook it over the front of the cockpit, making sure the release handle is outside and can be reached easily.

Canoes

There are some basic features that you should check for when choosing a canoe.

- Make sure you know which end is the front. Some models appear symmetrical at both ends but all have a bow and a stern.
- Consider whether you want to sit or kneel in your canoe and choose a model in which you feel comfortable doing that.
- Solo and double open canoes are available, as well as boats for three or more people. Doubles can be paddled by one person, but putting two people in a solo canoe is a recipe for a swim.
- End grabs may not be necessary because you can hold the seat or even the gunwale (upper edge of the hull).
- Padding around the seat is rarely needed because your legs can brace against or under the seat and on the inside of the boat, making your position more secure.

The design of the open canoe has changed very little since its invention.

An open canoe fitted with suitable equipment for use on white water.

Paddles

Kayak paddles have a blade at each end. Canoe paddles, in contrast, have only one blade and a T-grip at the other end, which is held in the top hand. Both kayak and canoe paddles come in a huge variety of shapes and sizes, and can be made from many different combinations of materials.

• The cheapest paddles will have plastic blades and a metal alloy shaft. They are commonly used for teaching beginners because they are inexpensive and fairly durable when used for low power, low-stress paddling. They are, however, heavy and invariably more difficult to use when compared with more expensive paddles.

• Wooden paddles can feel very nice, but they are rather high maintenance, since once the varnish is chipped they soak up water and become damaged. They are also fairly heavy, unless you buy one of the extremely expensive models.

• Composite paddles (carbon or moulded fibreglass) are light and strong, and they feel exquisite, but they are very expensive. They are probably the only type of paddle to deliver a really good flex pattern: this means the paddle is designed to flex enough to absorb shocks caused by impact with the water, but not enough to bend in a way that wastes energy or diminishes control. Most paddlers prefer stiff blades with some flex in the shaft.

Paddle Blades

When choosing a paddle you will find yourself faced with a range of shapes and sizes that may seem bewildering until you know what you are looking at.

Some paddles have "dihedral" faces, which means they have a raised spine on the drive face, sloping back either side. This adds strength and stiffness, but is mainly intended to stabilize the blade by allowing water to flow evenly off the face at each side. These paddles tend to be more powerful than spoon-shaped ones.

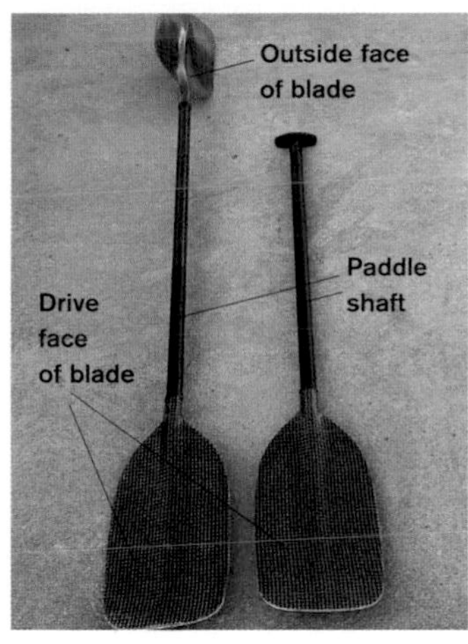

General-purpose kayak paddle (left) and the shorter canoe paddle.

Nineteenth-century wooden kayak paddle with no feather.

Paddles can have either symmetrical or asymmetrical blades. Asymmetrical blades are designed to enter the water more cleanly when forward paddling. They don't offer any significant benefits apart from this, and the disadvantage is that you can't use them either way around (you can use either side of a symmetrical blade). Beginners should choose a symmetrical blade.

In addition, a paddle can be feathered or unfeathered. Feather is the term used to describe the angle between the two blades on a kayak paddle. Many paddles are set at 90°, but the trend nowadays is for lesser angles of around 45°. The original reason for feather is so that the blade that isn't in the water doesn't present wind resistance. Hence, sea kayakers and racers use more feather.

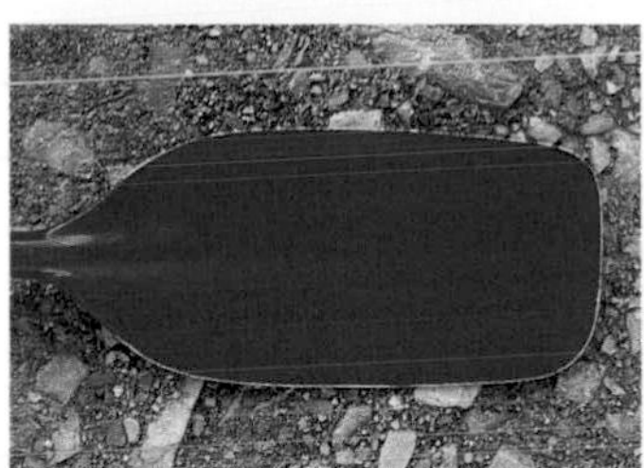

Clockwise from top left: paddle with reinforced metal edges used for white water paddling; asymmetrical paddle used for touring or racing; wing paddle used for racing; symmetrical paddle for general-purpose use.

Paddle Length

For beginners and general recreational paddling, the right length of paddle for you is determined by your height, and hence, your reach. The best way to check the length of a kayak paddle is to stand it up, level with your foot, and reach up and grasp the top blade. You should be able to do this comfortably with your arm only slightly bent.

With experience, paddlers tend to increase or decrease this length to suit their favourite type of paddling. White water paddles can be up to 20cm (8in) shorter than the general-purpose flat water kayak paddle, to give the paddler greater manoeuvrability. Open water and sea touring and racing paddles can be up to 10cm (4in) longer in order to give more power to each stroke.

A general-purpose canoe paddle is always shorter than a kayak paddle because it only has one blade. The T-grip of the canoe paddle should reach somewhere between your shoulder and your chin when the paddle is standing upright, level with your foot.

A bent paddle shaft (left) shown alongside a straight shaft.

Paddle Shaft

Usually the shaft of the paddle will be round, but some paddles have an oval section where the hands go, so that you can immediately feel which way the blade is facing. Canoe paddles achieve this by having a T-grip at the top, but the shaft is often oval-shaped in the area used by the bottom hand. Kayak paddles can be oval at the point where one or both of the hands take hold.

Typical length of a general-purpose kayak paddle for flat water.

Typical length of a white water kayak paddle: shorter for more control.

Typical length of a single-bladed flat water canoe paddle.

These lightweight white water paddles are extremely strong, and superior to heavier models.

Laminated wooden paddle. The wooden paddle can still compete with paddles made from man-made materials.

Split (break-down) paddles can be stored inside the kayak as spares in case of loss or breakage.

Some expensive paddles have bent shafts, which apply less stress to the wrists by loading them in a way that is more anatomically sound. Many paddlers used to straight-shafted paddles find that this feels a bit strange at first, but the concept is gradually gaining acceptance across all paddling disciplines.

Whichever type of paddle you first learn with, you will probably find that your personal style and anatomy, and your preferred type of paddling, dictate that you will soon want a longer or shorter paddle than these guidelines suggest.

Boaters will often be fiercely protective of their paddles, but if you are able to borrow the paddle of a friend before you buy your own, it will give you a better idea what differences a longer or shorter paddle, and the wide choice of shapes and constructions, can make to your paddling. If you are a member of a paddling club that supplies equipment, take the opportunity to test out different models. The sooner you can identify what works well for you and have a paddle that is exactly what you need, the faster your stroke skills will progress. But don't rush into it. Make sure you are comfortable with a paddle before you buy. Paddles can be expensive, and it is a good idea, if you can, to put off buying one for as long as possible. When you are sure what kind of paddling you want to practise, and have learned the basic strokes, you will be in a much better position to choose.

A replica of a traditional Greenland paddle, based on the Inuit style.

Traditional wooden canoe paddles. One has a reinforced square tip; the other is more suited to deep water.

Transporting your Boat

Most people need to move their boat about on land before they can use it on the water. How you do this will depend on the type of craft and how far you have to carry it. Broadly speaking, there are two options: carrying the boat manually, or mechanically.

Carrying the Boat

Many beginners will carry a boat between two people, using the end grabs. Two boats together can also be carried in this way. However, once you have become more familiar with carrying your boat, you might find it easier to carry a kayak or a light canoe on your shoulder. Carrying boats by holding on to the ends is the usual method for heavily laden craft.

When carrying a boat on your shoulder, you can either carry the paddle in your free hand, or you can put the paddle in the cockpit and carry the boat and the paddle together.

Boats that are too heavy to lift, such as a loaded sea kayak, can be moved short distances using a trolley. The trolley can be dismantled and transported in the boat while afloat.

A fold-up trolley is useful for moving large boats from the car to the launching point. The trolley can be dismantled and stowed on the boat during the trip.

Kayaks and canoes are now made from such lightweight materials that most adults are able to carry their boat on their back for short distances.

Two paddlers carry their loaded sea kayaks down to the water. Hold the boat's end grabs, one in each hand.

Transporting your Boat

Over longer distances, you may have to transport your boats by car or van, boat or aeroplane. The key here is to be sensible, and to think about whether your boat will get damaged, or could cause damage to other people's property.

A cockpit cover will allow you to put additional gear inside your boat. This is by far the best way to carry paddles and bulky safety and rescue equipment.

You will need a good roof rack if you are going to carry your boat on top of your car. Make sure the roof bars are securely attached to the car; if in doubt, tie the boat to the car as well.

Pad your roof rack with pipe lagging or proper pads bought for the purpose, and tie down the boat, using webbing roof straps with metal buckles. If you plan to carry more than two boats, it is worth getting upright bars to attach to the roof rack to enable you to carry up to six boats.

Don't be afraid to take your boat on a commercial flight or passage. Most companies will carry one piece of sports equipment per passenger free of charge. You just have to check the boat in with the rest of your luggage, and then take it over to the oversized baggage area. Always make sure it is well wrapped.

(Top right) Kayaks are best transported on their side, strapped firmly to the bars and uprights. It is much better to use proper roof straps than to tie the boat on with rope.

Do not tie kayaks on to roof racks right side up. They are unaerodynamic this way, and they will quickly fill with water if it rains.

The correct orientation for a single kayak if you are not using uprights on the roof rack. If carrying more than one boat, store them sideways.

A strong roof rack is essential. This one has uprights bolted to it, which are ideal for transporting kayaks.

The roof bars and uprights can be padded with proprietary roof bar pads or with pipe lagging, to protect the boats from damage during transit.

Make sure the boats are sensibly positioned and roughly centred fore and aft on the roofrack.

Essential Clothing

The right clothing is vital when you are on the water, not least because if you fall in and the conditions get cold, you could suffer remarkably quickly.

Before you get into a boat, you must consider what you should be wearing, some of which might be provided by your instructor. This will, to an extent, depend on the weather, but as a general rule you need to think about thermal insulation, in addition to footwear and flotation.

Insulation

Your insulation requirements will depend on the weather conditions you can expect to experience on the day you are boating. Always check the weather forecast before you set out, and adapt your level of clothing accordingly.

• If the climate is tropical and the water is warm, you do not need any insulation. You could paddle in a swimming costume, but some degree of sun protection is recommended. If the weather is balmy, you should have a T-shirt and shorts, and something warmer in case you capsize or swim, and get drenched. Whatever you wear should not get heavy when soaked; items made of polyester or polypropylene

Tight-fitting thermals are the best base layer in cold weather.

A thermal top worn with board shorts is ideal for warm weather.

A correctly fitting cagoule: close-fitting but allowing full upper body motion.

This cagoule is too big. It would be cold and difficult to swim or paddle in.

A flotation aid worn over the top of a cagoule and board shorts.

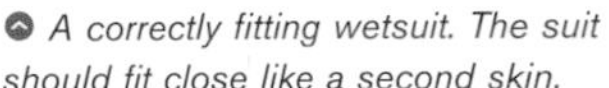

A correctly fitting wetsuit. The suit should fit close like a second skin.

An incorrectly fitting wetsuit. The baggy suit will not feel comfortable.

Wear waterproof trousers and a cagoule over thermals as an alternative to a wetsuit.

are better for warmth when wet than cotton. Board shorts, popular with surfers, are ideal for boating because they are durable for sliding in and out of the kayak or canoe, but do not soak up much water.

• If the water temperature is less than pleasant for dangling your fingers and toes in, or the air is a little too chilly for a T-shirt, then a thermal base layer is necessary. Choose one made from polyester fleece or polypropylene thermal material, or wear a wetsuit over your thermal layers. The wetsuit should be as close fitting as possible without being restrictive.

• If wind chill is an issue, you can add a wind- and spray-proof shell top over your thermals for upper body warmth. There is a wide variety available from water-sports suppliers, including wind-tops, spray-tops, paddling jackets or cagoules (also known as cags); different manufacturers give their products different names. The features to look for are waterproof fabric, neoprene cuffs, comfortable neck seal and an adjustable or elasticated waist.

Protective Headgear

Helmets are not a legal requirement but they should be worn whenever your experience and the conditions dictate that they are necessary. You are always safer wearing a helmet: if in doubt, wear one.

A correctly fitting helmet sits snugly on the head without sliding forward.

A helmet that is too small exposes the temples, giving no protection.

A helmet that is too big will expose the base of the skull and can impair vision.

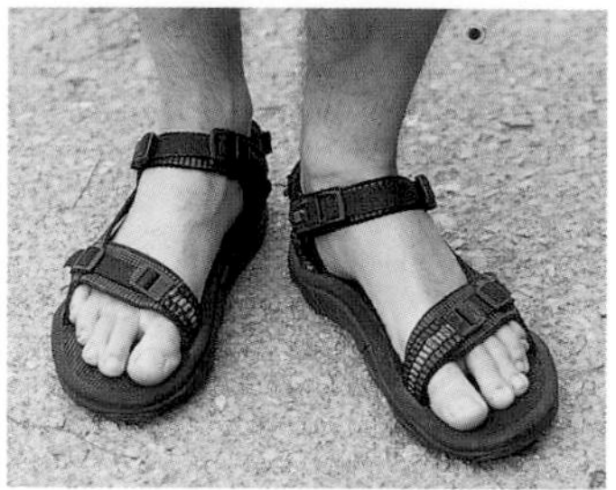

Technical sandals: lightweight and comfortable, and widely available.

Wetsuit boots make ideal footwear and will keep feet warm even when wet.

Specialist water-sports shoes make a good alternative to wetsuit boots.

Footwear

You cannot paddle well if you are wearing heavy, cumbersome footwear, although bare feet are not ideal either.

In most water environments it is a good idea to wear something on your feet. Old trainers (sneakers) or running shoes are often recommended, but they can be bulky and the rubber soles can jam on the inside of the boat.

If the weather is warm, technical sandals may be appropriate. These are comfortable, and are light enough to swim in should you capsize. They are also relatively inexpensive.

Otherwise, wetsuit boots are best, although they will add to the cost of kitting yourself out. Wetsuit boots are good to walk, scramble and swim in, they are unlikely to come off accidentally, and are warm as well as lightweight.

Specialist water-sport shoes are a good alternative to wetsuit boots. These have non-slip soles that are ideal for wet surfaces, and are padded and reinforced in all the right places. They often have straps to keep them firmly on the feet during a swim. Again, though, this is specialist footwear and not necessary for beginners starting out.

Flotation

A buoyancy or flotation aid (personal flotation device, also known as a PFD) is a vital piece of paddling equipment. Over-confident beginners might think that the buoyancy aid is surplus to their requirements, but no matter how strong a swimmer you are, you should always wear one when you are on the water. It is extremely rare for anyone to drown while kayaking or canoeing with a buoyancy aid; but unfortunately it does happen to those without them.

There are many different styles on the market, but the important thing is that it should be a buoyancy aid and not a life jacket, and that it should allow you to wave your arms about freely. It should fit well enough so that it does not pull up and off when you are in the water – check this does not happen by pulling up, or getting someone else to pull up, the shoulders. Also check that all the straps and fasteners do up properly.

In many countries there are stringent standards for what may be sold as a buoyancy aid. In Europe, look for the CE EN393 Approved Buoyancy Aid, and in the United States, the US Coastguard Approved Personal Flotation Device.

Flotation Maintenance

It is worth remembering that a buoyancy aid that is a few years old may not provide the expected level of flotation. It really does pay to look after your buoyancy aid correctly. Whether you are using your own buoyancy aid or one belonging to your paddling club, do not stand on it, sit on it or do anything else that might compress the foam, and make it less effective. Although wearing a buoyancy aid is never an absolute guarantee of your safety, it is essential that the buoyancy aid you wear will perform exactly as you expect it to.

A correctly adjusted flotation aid should fit snugly to the body.

Check the flotation aid cannot come off accidentally by pulling firmly upwards.

A reinforced neoprene spraydeck (skirt) for white water paddling. It has a tight-fitting body tube that is pulled right up to prevent water getting in.

A nylon spraydeck suitable for flat water paddling, but not rough water.

A cagoule is worn over the spraydeck to prevent water from splashing up and entering down the body tube.

A nylon spraydeck worn over a light sweater and board shorts is perfectly adequate for flat water paddling.

TIP

Spraydecks (skirts) are not needed on flat water because you are not likely to get a soaking from splashing water. However, if you do use one, it is essential that you know how to attach and remove it without help.

Fitness and Personal Skills

As with most sports, the fitter you are the more success you will have. When it comes to boating, being relatively fit and a competent swimmer are even more important for the sake of personal safety. You must also be able to set yourself clearly defined, achievable goals.

You need very little in the way of skills when you first begin to paddle, but the one essential is the ability to swim. You should be able to swim at least 50m (170ft) in the clothing you will be wearing when you paddle the boat. Only if reliable, trained rescue cover is forewarned and constantly at hand should a paddler who can not meet these basic standards go paddling, unless practising in the shallow end of a swimming pool.

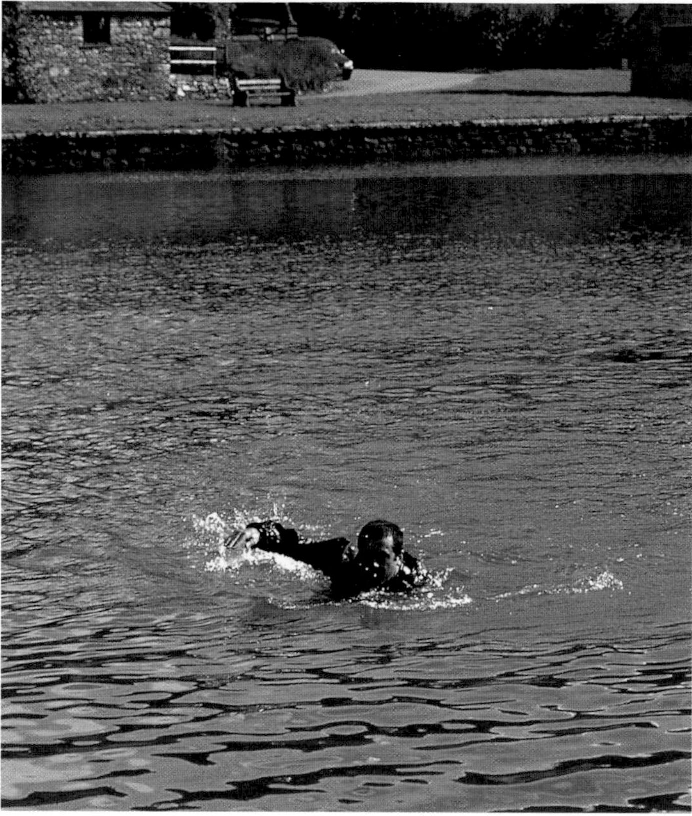

The ability to swim 50m (170ft) in the clothing you paddle in is essential.

Personal Fitness

One of the important activities most commonly overlooked by paddlers is their physical preparation for the demands of the sport. The demands will obviously be to a much higher degree if you are doing white water freestyle, but even if you are paddling around gently you need some kind of preparation. It will dramatically enhance the amount of fun you get from paddling, while simultaneously reducing the likelihood of injury and tiredness. After all, why tend aching muscles and stiff joints the day after you paddle, when you can so easily avoid them?

As you attempt more and more demanding kinds of paddling, or paddle further and in more exposed situations, you should have a level of strength and fitness commensurate with the challenge you are undertaking. This can only be acquired by practice and experience. Even extremely strong and athletic people find that they struggle when attempting to use their strength and fitness in unfamiliar ways or conditions.

Mental Fitness

Sportsmen and women now realize that their state of mind is as important as their physical condition. It does not matter what level they are at, whether professional or amateur, they still want to perform to the best of their ability.

The secrets of a good state of mind are feeling confident and positive, and clearly visualizing yourself realizing a set of achievable goals. Unless you believe you really can realize these goals, you will make it much harder for yourself to do so. Have a clear picture in your mind of what you plan to do. And having achieved those goals (or not!), set the next ones with an equal degree of realism.

The final stage of mental fitness is remembering to listen and be receptive. That does not just mean listening to your instructor. The most important thing is to listen to your body, and to be aware of yourself and the water. Never become so obsessed with what you have been told, or what you have read, that you focus on that more than upon vital, first-hand experience.

Special Needs Paddlers

Paddlers with disabilities (mental or physical) have particular needs that must be met if they are to realize their potential on the water with minimal risk and full enjoyment. The aim is to enable the special needs paddler to participate as far as possible with the same equipment and the same objectives as anybody else, with any modifications being made as required for that person. The key factor is good communication between the experienced paddler(s) leading the group, the paddler with special needs, his or her parents, and any medical and care staff. This will produce a paddling programme tailored to meet the needs of the individual.

Out of Water Training

Knowing the ins and outs of keeping fit, and avoiding injury, apply as much to paddlers as to any other sportsmen and women. Being fit also enables you to achieve your goals; you cannot paddle if your muscles are aching and tired.

All-body Workouts

Many people use paddling as their main form of exercise, and paddling vigorously or over a long distance is certainly an excellent, all-body workout. Despite the fact that your legs do not appear to be doing much, they are actually contributing quite a lot of the power, provided you have a good paddling technique. If you want to progress with your boating skills, however, you may want to do extra, non-paddling exercises to tone your muscles and increase body strength.

Running is good cardiovascular exercise, but beware of impact.

Swimming provides an excellent body workout without straining muscles.

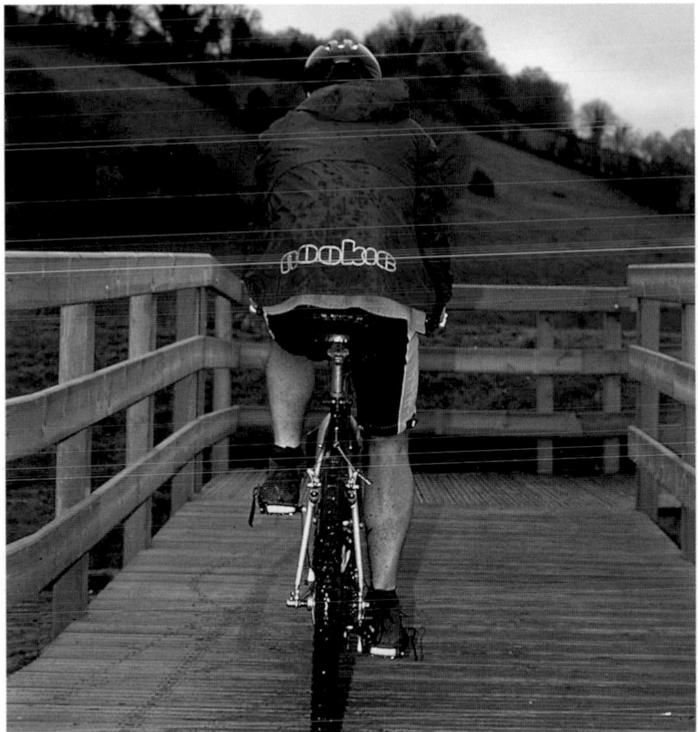

Cycling is good training for the quads, the large, powerful muscles in the thighs.

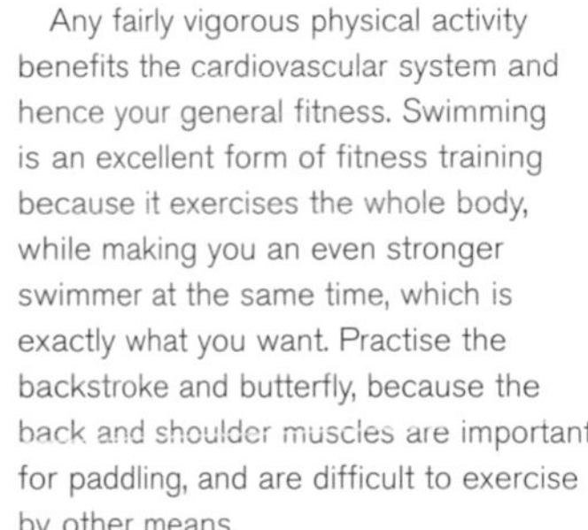

Any fairly vigorous physical activity benefits the cardiovascular system and hence your general fitness. Swimming is an excellent form of fitness training because it exercises the whole body, while making you an even stronger swimmer at the same time, which is exactly what you want. Practise the backstroke and butterfly, because the back and shoulder muscles are important for paddling, and are difficult to exercise by other means.

Cycling and running are good for improving all-round fitness, and are especially good for the quadriceps (the big thigh muscles), which are used a surprising amount when paddling. Much of the torso rotation in a forward paddling stroke comes from the quadriceps.

Many paddlers favour either climbing or snowboarding as a second sport, whether because of a love of the outdoors or because they are extremely complementary disciplines. Whatever cross-training you choose to do, use it in moderation and aim for a good all-round level of fitness. Regular gentle exercise – every day, if possible – will help you avoid illness and injury.

Targeted Action

If you have access to a gym, then a professionally planned regime can target the muscle groups you need to exercise.

Avoid concentrating too much on the arm muscles because the quadriceps, abdominals, shoulder and back muscles do most of the work when you are in the boat. The arms mainly provide fine motor control, and gain more from activities such as juggling than from lifting weights.

Press-ups, pull-ups and crunches are the best simple non-gym exercises to prepare you for paddling, and these are all something you can do at home.

Avoiding Injury

Whichever exercises you do, remember that it is vitally important to warm up first, and then to stretch, or you might strain or pull a muscle. It is also important to make sure that your posture is correct when exercising. Kayakers, in particular, are prone to lower back problems if they fail to keep their spinal curvature correct.

After any form of exercise you must also stretch again and warm down. This helps keep injuries at bay. It might seem wholly unnecessary, but it pays dividends. It also gives you time to focus on how you have performed, and how you can improve next time. Mental visualization is extremely important, and will make more difference to your paddling than almost any other single factor.

Good Habits

If you can integrate exercise into your daily life it will save you a lot of time and money that you might otherwise spend on fitness clubs and sports equipment. Simply being more aware of your body will help you enormously. For example, by knowing which muscle groups are working to perform different actions, you may find yourself doing a mini workout just walking up the stairs.

Maintaining a good body posture at all times, whether exercising, at work in the office or watching television at home, will also make a difference. Your posture can affect both your performance as a paddler and your overall well-being. Not only will you find it easier to make more effective strokes in your boat, you will also reduce the risk of injury, particularly damage to your back.

The press-up is an exercise to build short, powerful muscles in the pectoral, bicep and tricep areas of the body.

You may find that by supporting your weight with your knees, you will find it easier to do more repetitions.

Diagonal crunches (elbow to knee) are excellent training for paddling.

Pull-ups mimic paddling exceptionally well and help to promote arm strength.

Warming Up

You should always warm up before you do any kind of strenuous activity. Warming up is essential to prepare your body for sudden exertions and to minimize the risk of injury. Your body will then be much more flexible and able to absorb shocks and over-extensions. Even stretching should not be attempted until you have warmed up thoroughly.

Establish a Routine

It is important to formulate a pre-paddling routine for yourself, and to make a habit of following it as a precursor to going out on the water.

Start with some light warm-up exercise for at least 15 minutes. Depending on how often you go out paddling, you might want to include a selection of activities in your routine, so that you don't become bored with the same one.

Once you have warmed up, it is time for some gentle stretching. This can improve the performance of your muscles and tendons enormously and, at the same time, it will dramatically reduce the likelihood of injury.

Practise the body stretches given over the following pages to achieve a good all-round level of flexibility. Do not bounce to increase your range of movement, but extend yourself gently to the limit of comfort and hold each stretch for about 15 seconds before relaxing.

Next, get into your boat, still on land, and continue with the boat stretching exercises. You can then take the boat stretches one step further by going out on to the water. This will ensure that everything has been stretched in the right way, and that there are no problems with your range and freedom of movement.

After paddling for a while, it is often beneficial to stop your boat and repeat the in-boat stretches. Remember, too, that it is important to warm down and stretch once again after you have finished paddling and are back on land.

Simulated paddling action on land can make sure everything is moving properly without any undue strain.

Gentle jogging, especially through water, is a great way to warm up.

How to Warm Up

The best way to warm up is with gentle exercise. This could take the form of walking briskly, particularly uphill, with your arms swinging. If the water is warm, then you could have a warm-up swim. Some people like to play with a frisbee, and this sort of group activity can be a lot of fun, and adds to the enjoyment of the whole occasion.

In fact, any activity is fine, provided you actually feel yourself getting warm, and your heart rate is raised significantly. You should be able to sense this without taking your pulse. Do not go for a fast run to warm up though, or do anything that involves impact because it could be counter-productive.

Body Stretches

Light stretches are a vital part of your warm-up routine. They help fine-tune the body, can be done in the home or on the river bank or beach, and are a good way of building up team spirit when done in a group. There are a variety of simple stretches you can do to ensure that you have extended every muscle group in your body, and you will not require any props or assistance to do them.

Gentle neck rotation to the left and to the right is a good way to start off your stretching routine.

Neck flexion. Bend the head forward from the neck, but do not rotate or roll the head, which is bad for the spine.

Spine extension.

Hamstring, tricep and shoulder stretch.

Quadriceps and hamstring stretch.

General arm and shoulder stretch.

Trunk rotation stretch.

Side stretch.

Stretching in the Boat

After your initial stretches on land, it is time to get seated in the boat and continue your warm-up routine with exercises that simulate more closely your movements while out on the water.

Before Getting Afloat

Exercises performed in the boat while you are still on land serve a dual purpose. First, you will be getting all the usual benefits of stretching, but specifically geared to the range of motion you have in the boat. Second, you are checking that you have good freedom of movement in the boat and in your paddling kit. If something is hurting, chafing or digging into your ribs when you do these stretches, get out now and solve the problem immediately.

On the Water

Once you have warmed up, stretched, and are afloat, it is a good idea to go for a bit of a paddle to settle into your boat, and then do some more stretching, perhaps using the paddle as an additional prop. There are a number of useful exercises that anyone can do without risk of capsizing, and they are all good confidence-building tools for new or nervous paddlers.

Having done all this preparation, you are now ready to paddle more skilfully and effectively than someone who jumps straight into the boat without first warming up and stretching. Typically, the whole process would take about 30 minutes, but it is time well spent. Without this pre-paddling routine, you probably would not be able to spend as much time on the water, and your skill and fitness levels might well stagnate.

TIPS

- Always stretch gently and progressively; never bounce.
- Only use your muscles to stretch; do not use weights or external forces, which will cause muscle strain and possible injury.
- If you stretch to the point that it hurts, you have over-reached yourself and should stop the stretch.

Boat Stretches on Land

1 Make sure you can reach the right-hand side of the stern with your left hand.

2 Repeat the same stretch on the other side of the boat, using your right hand.

3 Extend fully backwards, so that you are stretching over the back deck.

4 Then, extend fully forwards, so that you are stretching over the front deck.

Boat Stretches on Water

1 Press the left blade against the right-hand side of the bow and vice versa.

2 Press the left blade against the right-hand side of the stern and vice versa.

3 Stretch forward in the boat as far as you can and hold for a few seconds.

4 Stretch backwards in the boat as far as you can and hold for a few seconds.

Dagger

KAYAKING SKILLS

Kayaking and canoeing are accessible to most people because the skills required to get in the boat and have fun are not specialized. If, however, you want to progress in one area of the sport, or want to paddle for longer distances or look after friends and family while they, too, enjoy their paddling, you ought to acquire some new skills.

This section outlines the basic skills and strokes that will help you to use the boat in a skilful manner. The exercises are described in approximately the order in which they tend to arise, although some instructors may prefer a different order.

When you are learning how to do each technique, try not to progress too fast. Make sure you have the right skills in place before you move on. Equally, though, it is a bad idea to practise a technique badly. If something is not working and you do not know why, change to a different skill until you can find out how to deal with your problem. Sometimes just going away and trying again much later is all it takes.

Choose a sheltered piece of flat water near to the shore to try out these skills. Put safety first, and make sure you are confident that you can swim to a safe landing place and rescue your equipment. This is a simple point, but so often overlooked.

A group of paddlers under instruction, using short general-purpose kayaks.

Practising a reverse sweep stroke. Head and body rotation are part of good technique.

Getting into the Kayak

The first thing to learn is how to get into your kayak when it is afloat. If it is a sit-on or an open cockpit boat, this is a simple enough matter, but a closed cockpit kayak (where your legs are under the deck) can be more difficult. You can practise on dry land if your boat is reasonably sturdy, but sooner or later you'll have to try it on water.

Find a place to launch where the bank or jetty is not too much higher than the gunwale of your kayak. Place the boat on the surface of the water here, making sure that the water is sufficiently deep that you will still be afloat after you get in! If it is deep enough to capsize, ensure that it is also deep enough to get out of the boat when upside down.

Don't be tempted to tether the boat to the bank, which would make things very difficult if you capsized. It may be possible to step into the boat while holding on to the bank, simply pick up your paddle, and paddle away, but this can often be tricky. A useful technique is to place your paddle across the boat at the back of the cockpit, and hold on to it and the cockpit rim at the same time. The paddle blade will then be resting on the bank, and this will stop the boat floating away, as well as supporting the back deck of the boat – some kayaks are not strong enough to be sat on without a little reinforcement.

Don't attempt this if the bank is much higher than the kayak, or you just will tip yourself in: find another launch place.

Now that the boat is afloat and you are holding on to it and the paddle, place one foot in the bottom of the boat, and make sure it is right in the middle before you put any weight on it. Transfer all your weight on to that foot and, still holding on to boat and paddle with one hand, place your other foot right inside the footwell of the boat and sit down on the back deck. Take a moment to get settled.

You may now need to change hand positions, but from here you should be able to lift yourself up again and move forward to sit down on the seat. With luck or practice you are still holding the paddle behind you, and have your other hand free to help you stabilize your position without being cast adrift. Sit centrally on the seat and arrange your clothing and equipment in an orderly fashion.

Finally, get your legs into position in the cockpit. Now you are ready to use your free hand to hold on to the bank, and can bring your paddle around in front of you ready to paddle away.

Getting into the Kayak

1 Place the boat in the water as close to the river bank as possible. Keep hold of the cockpit to stop the boat drifting off.

2 Place the paddle across the back of the cockpit. Continue to hold on to the front of the cockpit with your left hand.

3 Put one leg at a time into the boat. Steady yourself and the boat by holding on to the bank and the boat.

4 Slide forward into the cockpit and get both legs in. You should still be holding on to the paddle and the river bank.

5 Bend your knees to get both your legs stretched out beneath the front deck. Continue to hold the paddle and the bank.

6 Adjust your position so that you are sitting comfortably on the seat. Bring the paddle to the front and you are ready.

Seating Position

Sloppy posture is bad at any time, but doubly so when paddling because it puts a strain on your back, and can lead to all sorts of problems, some of which can mean long-term damage. The following tips spell out exactly how you should sit to avoid injury.

In most kayaks there will be a seat, which, with the position of the backrests and footrests, will dictate which way you are supposed to face. What is not so obvious is the correct posture.

Maintaining good spinal posture means keeping your back straight and shoulders back, so that your spine is curved like the letter S: imagine you were sitting on an upright chair. If you do not, you will not be able to paddle properly. If your kayak is equipped with a back strap, the strap will give support and will encourage you to sit up properly. Even without this support though, you should be able to maintain a good, upright posture.

A common mistake is to slouch against the back of the cockpit. New paddlers often do this from the start, and even after you know how to sit there is a tendency to do this when tired. But if you cannot sit up properly in the boat, it is time to get out. By slouching, you make every stroke more difficult and less effective, and it is very bad for your back.

In most kayaks you will sit with your knees under the deck and your legs bent, so that pressing the feet against the footrest will push your knees up and out to maintain a firm grip on the boat. In some racing and fast touring boats the paddler will sit with the knees straight up, but in the majority of kayaks this does not afford good control.

Sometimes people worry that they will not be able to get out of the boat if they capsize because their legs are under the deck. This is not actually a problem, but worrying about it is, so practise getting out until you have allayed your fears.

Correct seating position in a kayak. The knees are under the deck, and the body is upright and central.

Incorrect seating position. The knees should not be bent up in this particular type of kayak.

Correct seating position for a narrow, racing kayak, which is designed to be paddled with the knees up.

Correct posture. The body is upright, maintaining a well-defined spinal "S".

Incorrect posture. Slouching backwards may cause spinal injury.

The release handle of the spraydeck (skirt) should be visible and within reach.

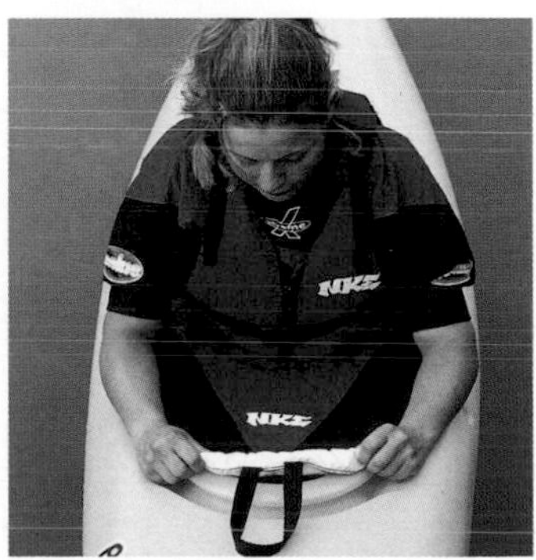

Capsize Drill in a Kayak

You cannot get into a boat unless you accept that you may capsize. Hence, you also need to learn the escape drill. It is a simple skill, but the sooner you learn it the better. Losing the fear of capsizing means you will enjoy paddling a lot more.

Most people realize that a kayak, by its very nature, is prone to capsize. Although this can be avoided, the beginner will not know how, and that is why everyone should know how to capsize.

If you try to get out of a kayak while it is in the process of capsizing, you run the risk of injuring yourself or ending up in a position where your head is underwater, but you cannot free yourself. It is better to wait until the boat has capsized and stopped moving, and then get out. It is quite hard to visualize what you will do when you are upside down, but do not worry. When you are in the water you will not be aware of being upside down. Everything will look and feel exactly as it does when upright, except, of course, that you will be holding your breath.

First, remove your spraydeck (spray skirt), if you are wearing one, by pulling up the release handle and letting go. Then, bang on the bottom or sides of the boat to attract attention. Lean forwards and push yourself out by placing your hands either side of the cockpit. You will naturally do a somersault in the water, breaking surface in front of the cockpit.

If you come up directly under the boat, do not worry because kayaks are so narrow that there is no way you will be stuck underneath. If you can open your eyes it helps, but you can easily escape blind. If possible, try to keep hold of your paddle, but this is often difficult. As soon as your head breaks surface, take hold of the boat and paddle or swim to the bow or stern. From there you can swim the boat ashore. Alternatively, someone may rescue you and help you back to land, or put you back in your boat so that you can continue paddling.

You should practise the capsize drill every time you go kayaking, until you are extremely confident. Most people do it at the end of a session because emptying a boat is tiring, and you need to be fully warmed up before you do it. If you get cold doing a capsize drill at the end of a session, imagine what it would have been like to capsize at the beginning.

With practice, you may be able to keep hold of the boat with one hand, and the paddle with the other. This can be very useful to rescuers, or if you need to try to get back in the boat on your own. In practice, however, a paddler with these skills will be ready to learn how to roll as an alternative to capsizing, and will be determined to stay in the boat.

Capsize and Get Out (underwater view)

1 Locate the spraydeck (skirt) release handle and pull off the spraydeck.

2 Bring your knees together, place your hands on each side and tuck forwards.

3 Push firmly away with your hands and you will fall out of the boat easily.

4 From the cockpit, turn to one side. Hold on to the boat and paddle if you can.

TIPS

- Wait until the boat has capsized completely before you try to get out of the boat.
- Pull off your spraydeck (spray skirt) as a matter of urgency, using the handle at the front of the boat.
- Make sure your spraydeck has been released all the way around the cockpit before you attempt to move, or you risk getting caught up in it.
- Free both of your knees from under the deck at the front of the boat.
- Tuck your body forwards, with your knees pulled up to your chest in a foetal position; don't try to lie across the back deck.
- Aim to keep hold of your boat with one hand as you come up to the surface of the water.
- Don't try to get your head above the surface of the water until your legs are completely out of the boat because you risk getting into a tangle that could prove dangerous: learn the stages of a capsize in one sequence and keep to it.

Capsize and Get Out (above water view)

1 You are on flat water and are ready to begin the capsize drill. Keep your hands by your sides and take a deep breath.

2 Lean over to one side and capsize. At first, you may have to resist your body's natural instinct to right itself.

3 Remain sitting upright, at 90° to the boat, as you go over. It may help to place your hands on the sides of the boat.

4 It will help to keep hold of the sides of the boat as your head hits the water and goes under.

5 Wait in this position until the boat stops moving. You will feel it settle when you are completely upside down.

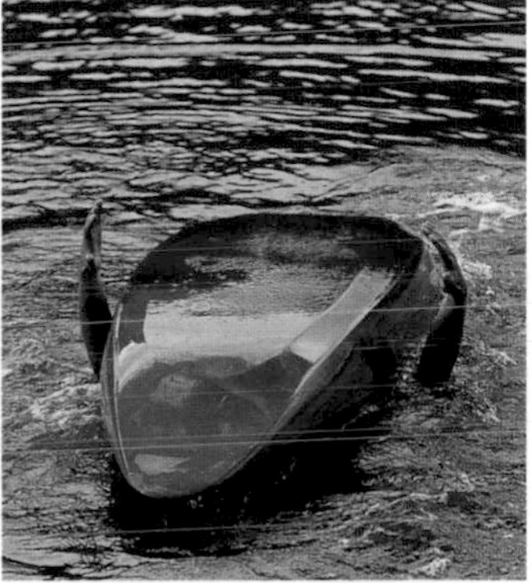

6 Once completely inverted, bang on the bottom or sides of the boat. This makes a loud noise and attracts attention.

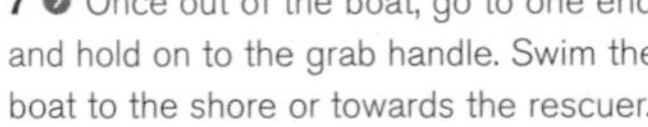

7 ➋ Once out of the boat, go to one end and hold on to the grab handle. Swim the boat to the shore or towards the rescuer.

TIPS

- Only practise the capsize drill when there is an instructor or experienced rescuer on hand to help you in case you get into difficulties.
- Make sure the water is at least 1.2m (4ft) deep. It is tempting to stay in shallow water, but this can lead to entrapment or injury.

Holding the Paddle

How the paddle is held is critical if you are going to use it properly. This is because the correct grip enables the paddler to apply the maximum amount of force with the minimum effort. It is also important to hold the paddle in the same way every time you pick it up. Reacting to the signals the paddle sends you from the water is an important part of paddling, and you can only learn to interpret that feedback if you have a consistent grip.

Almost all kayak paddles are feathered (one blade at an angle to the other), which means that with each stroke you will turn the paddle to put the other blade in the water. One hand will be your control hand and will grip the paddle at all times. Allow the paddle shaft to turn in the other, non-control hand, gripping it only as you make the stroke on that side.

Find your best hand position by putting the middle of the paddle shaft on your head and shuffling your hands until your elbows make 90°, making sure that your hands are still equidistant from the blades when you have finished.

Hold the paddle out in front of you with your arms straight and horizontal, knuckles up. Grip the paddle with your control hand so that the blade on this side is vertical, and the drive (concave) face is forward. If it is your paddle, you can mark the hand positions with tape. Now you are ready to paddle.

Never be tempted to change your grip on the paddle once you've got it right. There are no significant advantages to shifting your grip, and you will find that any changes hamper the learning process. Learning is feedback-related. You do something, you feel the effect; you do it a bit differently, and you feel a different effect. Changing your grip means you have to start out all over again.

You will get used to the feather angle of your paddle. Beginners often ask why kayak paddles can't be flat: the reason is so that the blade that isn't in the water doesn't give wind resistance as it goes through the air. Once you are used to it, a change in feather will feel strange to you. This is one reason why you should try to use the same paddle if you can.

A good way to find the correct grip is to put the paddle on your head, with your hands equidistant from each end and your elbows at 90°.

TIPS

- The control hand's grip on the paddle never changes during a stroke; instead, the wrist of the control hand is flexed.
- The slip hand loosens between strokes to allow the shaft to rotate.

Incorrect hold. You should never hold the paddle shaft off-centre.

Incorrect hold. Here, the hands are too close together on the shaft.

Make sure that when your arms are pointing straight up, the blade on the control side is facing down towards the water.

Using the Paddle

There is more to paddling than building up a fantastic set of arm muscles, and thrashing about. Good paddling is an art, and that means following certain rules.

With all paddle strokes you should aim to put the whole of the blade in the water, but no more. There is no advantage to the blade being deeper in the water, and it will not work properly if it is only half in. The whole blade should be just immersed.

When you make a stroke, you should always try to rotate your shoulders to give you as much reach as possible. This also means that much of the power for the stroke will come from your leg and torso muscles, leaving your relatively smaller arm muscles to provide control and react to feedback during the stroke. It is a misconception to think that kayaking is exclusively about using your arms. In fact, with good technique, a vigorous workout is much more likely to leave you with tired and aching legs and stomach muscles.

The other point that a kayak paddler should concentrate on is head rotation. Before making a stroke you should make sure your head is facing in the direction you want the boat to move in. So, for forward paddling, you must be looking at the horizon. If you want to turn the boat to the left or right, you should first turn your head to look that way. This helps the whole of your body make the strokes. It also tends to inhibit various bad practices, such as looking at the paddle blades or the end of your boat, neither of which are any help and will encourage bad posture, which can lead to injury.

Using the paddle properly is essential to make each of your strokes count.

Correct technique: the paddle blade is submerged just deep enough to start a forward stroke.

Blade too deep in the water – the paddler's hand is too low.

Blade too shallow in the water – only half the blade would come into play.

Forward Paddling

A good forward paddling stroke is a basic requirement, but it is not the easiest stroke to master. The main aim is to propel the boat forward while applying as little turning force as possible. Normally, if you make a stroke on one side, the boat will move forwards while turning away from the paddle blade that made the stroke. In order to minimize this effect, you should make the stroke as close to the boat as possible, with the paddle shaft as upright as possible.

Reach forward as far as you can, leaning from the hips but without bending your spine forward. You should be able to put the blade in the water about 2.5cm (1in) from the boat, near your feet, and drive face back. When the blade is fully immersed, pull it back using your shoulders and torso, straightening up your top arm to push the "air blade" to the side of the boat that the stroke is on. This will make the paddle vertical and a lot more comfortable for you.

Continue to pull the paddle blade through the water until it is level with the back of the seat. Try to resist the urge to pull with your bottom arm for as long as possible. When your arm finally does bend at the elbow, it will be time to extract the blade from the water. Keep this blade the same distance from the boat throughout the stroke.

As soon as the blade is out of the water, rotate your body the other way to make the next stroke on the other side. As you do so, you will have to rotate the shaft with your control hand; drop in the blade with the drive face pointing the same way as before.

TIPS

- Remember that good forward paddling depends on three criteria:
    1. trunk rotation
    2. arm extension
    3. trunk rotation and arm extension and recovery of the blade being done as a smooth and continuous action.
- Lean forward to increase your reach.
- Rotate your body to the side on which you are placing the blade.
- Do as much of the stroke as you can with your arms straight.
- Watch paddlers who you know have a good technique and copy them.
- Practise your body movements when you are out of the water.

Forward Paddling Technique

1 Begin the forward stroke by placing the blade as far forward in the water as you comfortably can do.

2 Drop the whole of the blade into the water and start to push away from you with your top hand.

3 The blade in the water follows the side of the boat, and the bottom arm stays fairly straight.

4 As the water blade passes your body, the top arm should be coming across in front of your face.

5 Finally, as you reach the end of the stroke, the air blade starts to come down towards the water.

6 Continuing this motion recovers the water blade, and you are ready to place the opposite blade in the water.

About to make a stroke. Note that the top arm is bent, ready to punch the top blade forward.

Good forward paddling technique. The paddle is quite vertical and the blade is submerged.

Excellent body rotation, as the paddler is about to place the left blade in the water for another stroke.

Forward paddling on flat water in a general purpose kayak.

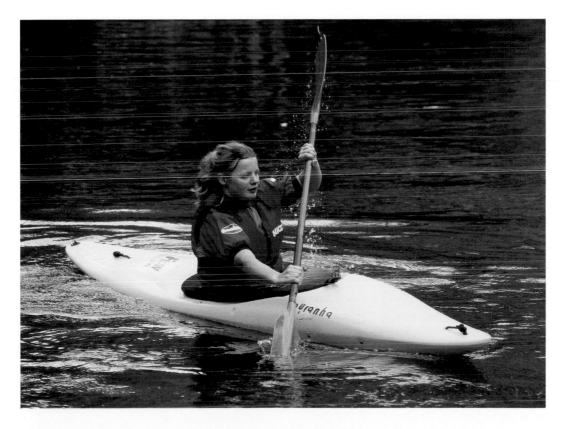

Backward Paddling

Paddling backwards is in principle no different from paddling forwards, but it is more difficult to get the hang of.

Do not change your grip on the paddle: this is a classic mistake made by most beginners. Always back-paddle using the back of the blade. There is no need to turn the paddle around since its curvature actually helps you to make the back stroke, and because it is bad practice to change your grip.

It is not possible to keep the paddle shaft as vertical as you do for forward paddling, or to keep the blades so close to the boat, but this is what you should aim for. Make a big effort to rotate your shoulders as far as you can to place the blade behind you – this also helps you to glance behind and see where you are going. Push your paddle forward through the water with your arms fairly straight, and make the stroke as long as you can.

Most boats will turn during the back stroke so that you zig-zag a little. Find somewhere where you will not crash into anything, and see how long you can keep going backwards in a straight line. It will teach you excellent control over the boat.

TIPS

- Think before you back-paddle: it may be quicker and easier to turn your boat and paddle forwards.
- Look over your shoulder at least every other stroke to avoid a crash.
- Pick out a feature behind you in the direction of travel, and focus on it whenever you turn around.

Incorrect method. Do not turn the paddle around like this.

Backward Paddling Technique

1 Rotate as far as you can to one side, and place the blade quite far back in the water behind the boat.

2 Drive the blade forwards through the water using your torso; do not use your arms for strength.

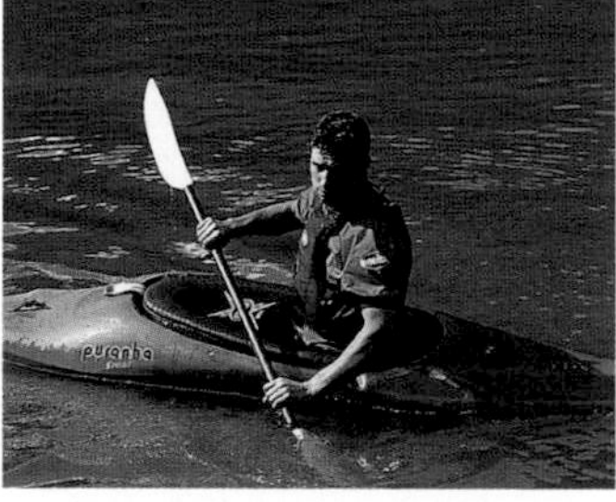

3 As you come around to face the front, straighten your arms, keeping the blade as close as you can to the boat.

4 Try to keep looking behind you as you finish the stroke. This may seem difficult at first but it will come with practice.

5 The stroke should end with the bottom arm straight and the blade in the area of the boat next to your feet.

6 As the blade comes out of the water, you can continue rotating to place the blade behind you on the other side.

Stopping

Learning how to stop the boat quickly is important. Use this stroke if you are in danger of hitting something.

Begin by moving the boat forwards at a good pace. To stop, jab one blade into the water next to your body, as if to paddle backwards. The drive face should be pointing backwards with the shaft perpendicular. Resist the force on the blade, but as soon as you tense against that force and the boat begins to turn, jab the other blade in quickly on the other side. Repeat on the first side, and by the time you make your fourth jab, the boat should have stopped. Do the jabs quite aggressively, and switch sides when you feel the pressure on the back of the blade.

Stopping quickly in a fast racing kayak requires sharp jabs in the water.

Stopping Technique

1 Jab the paddle in on one side, at 90° to the kayak rather than as you would for a normal stroke.

2 Pull the paddle out again as soon as you feel the pressure of the water on the blade and the boat begins to turn.

3 Drop the opposite blade in on the other side. Resist for a little longer this time, until the boat is pointing straight again.

4 Back on the side of the boat on which you started, make a longer back stroke this time.

5 Moving backwards this time, make a final stroke to straighten up the boat.

6 At the finish, you should be pointing in the same direction you were at the previous step, except with the boat still.

Forward Sweep Stroke

The forward sweep is the most useful turning stroke in the kayaker's repertoire. It will turn the boat on the spot, and can be used to turn the boat through 180°. By inserting just one sweep stroke, you can also change or correct your direction while paddling forwards, without breaking your rhythm.

Start by placing the blade in the water as far forward as possible, with the shaft fairly low and the drive face pointing away from the boat. Rotate your head and shoulders, so that they are facing the direction of travel. Keeping your bottom arm straight, sweep the paddle in as wide an arc as you can. When you have turned as far as you need to, or the blade is coming close to hitting the back of the boat, lift the blade straight out of the water – don't let it hit the boat.

It helps considerably if you can "edge" the boat slightly, so that the side opposite your stroke is raised a little for the first half of the stroke. Level the boat again as the paddle passes perpendicular to the kayak, or you may catch the paddle.

TIPS

- Practise edging the boat by lifting up one of your knees.
- The bigger the arc, the more effectively you will turn the boat.
- Think about the difference between a forward paddling stroke (vertical paddle, close to the boat) and a sweep stroke (low paddle, wide arc).
- Use the forward sweep if you want to turn while travelling forwards.

The forward sweep stroke is the most valuable turning stroke. It can be used to spin or to change direction.

Forward Sweep Technique

1 Place the paddle in the water as far forward as you can reach, with the blade facing away from the boat.

2 Keeping your lower arm straight, swing your paddle blade away from the front of the boat.

3 Looking in the direction you want to turn, continue to sweep the blade in the widest arc you can make.

4 Still looking where you want to go, continue to sweep until the blade is swinging in towards the stern.

5 At this point, quickly flip the blade up out of the water before it catches on the back of the boat and trips you up.

6 If you keep the boat stable and the blade out of the water, you'll carry on turning even after the stroke is finished.

Reverse Sweep Stroke

As the name implies, the reverse sweep stroke is the exact opposite of the forward sweep. It is a much more powerful turning stroke, but it should not be used while moving forwards unless you want to turn and head back in the other direction because it will arrest all forward motion.

Start with the paddle blade as far back as you can reach, on the side you want to turn towards. Rotate your head and shoulders in this direction. Drop the blade into the water with the drive face towards the boat, then sweep the blade forwards in the widest arc you can, until you are pointing the right way, or until the blade is about to hit the front of the boat. Lift the blade straight up out of the water.

Keep your bottom arm as straight as you can throughout the stroke, and try to keep the boat level in the water.

Incorrect technique: don't turn the paddle around. Use the back of the blade for all reverse strokes.

It should be easy to turn most general-purpose boats through 180° with one reverse sweep. Once the blade is out of the water, the kayak will continue to spin for further rotations. Practise spinning using alternate forward and reverse sweep strokes. Go forward on the left and reverse on the right to turn clockwise. Go forward on the right, then reverse on the left to spin in the opposite direction.

TIPS

- Use the back of the paddle blade and don't change your grip.
- Use a reverse sweep stroke when you need to make a powerful turn.
- Keep the boat fairly level in the water for a reverse sweep stroke.
- Remember, a reverse sweep stroke will arrest forward progress.
- Practise combining forward sweep strokes and reverse sweep strokes on opposite sides of the boat.

Reverse Sweep Technique

1 Rotate your body and look where you want the boat to be pointing. Place the blade in the water close to the stern, with the drive face towards the boat.

2 Sweep the blade out and forward, keeping the bottom arm straight. Note how the body hasn't actually moved but the boat has.

3 Complete the arc, leaning your body forward over the front deck to extend your reach as far as you can at the front of the boat.

4 Lift the paddle blade out of the water before it reaches the boat, or you will risk catching your paddle under the boat.

5 Keep the boat level and the blade out of the water, and keep looking where you want to go!

6 The boat continues turning on its own. It is usually possible to complete a 180° turn like this in general-purpose boats.

Draw Stroke

This stroke moves the boat through the water sideways, and although you can get by without being very good at it, learning to do it well will help you to improve many of your other skills. The draw stroke is, curiously, a fairly obscure technique that many paddlers never learn to do properly.

Place the blade in the water as far from the side of the kayak as you can reach, with the drive face pointing towards the boat. Push your top arm out as far as you can, so that the paddle shaft is as vertical as possible. Lift the edge of the kayak with your knee on the stroke side, and pull the blade towards your body. This should pull a general-purpose boat about 50cm (20in) sideways.

As the blade approaches, cock your wrists back quickly to rotate the blade 90°, then slice it back to where it started. If you do not, and the blade hits the boat, you may be knocked off balance or fall in. If you try to stop the stroke before it hits the hull, the same may happen.

From the starting position, straighten your wrists so that the paddle is pointing towards the boat, and repeat the stroke. If the boat turns rather than moves sideways, the stroke is being made too far towards the front or the back of the boat. If the bow starts to turn towards the paddle, move the stroke back a little, or vice versa for the stern. It can be very useful to make this happen deliberately though, so practise doing draw strokes towards the bow or stern.

Draw Stroke Technique

1 Rotate your body to face the way you want to move. Place the blade as far out to the side as you can, with the drive face towards the boat.

2 Pull the blade towards the boat, keeping the paddle as vertical as you can. Lifting your knee on the paddle side of the boat will help you achieve this.

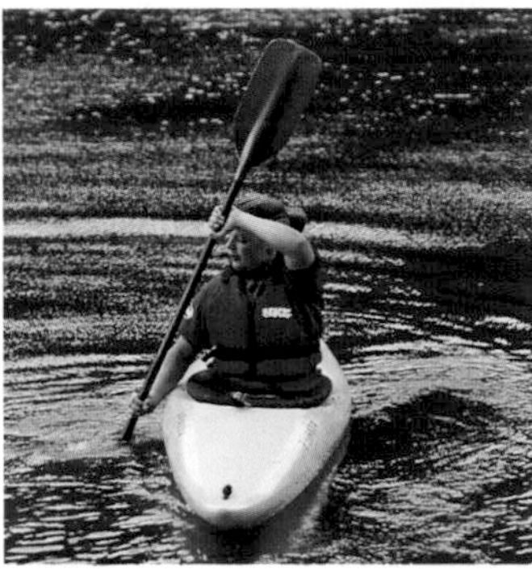

3 Continue to pull smoothly until the paddle blade is just about to reach the boat at a point level in the water with your hip.

4 Turn your wrists sharply through 90° to change the angle of the blade before it hits the boat.

5 Move the paddle away from the boat by slicing the blade out sideways to where it first started.

6 Flick your wrists back to their original position, so that the drive face is towards the boat. Repeat as required.

Sculling Draw

Like the draw stroke, the sculling draw will move the boat sideways. It has the advantage, however, of being more useful in a confined space. For instance, when you are close to a jetty and want to move closer, the draw stroke may be difficult to execute. The sculling draw is also a lot less likely to tip you in, although it is more difficult to do effectively.

Start with the paddle blade next to your hip, 20cm (8in) from the boat, with the shaft vertical and the drive face towards the hull. Cock your wrist so that the blade rotates 20°, opening out towards the bow.

Keep the shaft vertical and move the paddle forwards as far as you can. Keep the paddle 20cm (8in) from the boat, resisting its tendency to slice away from the hull. If anything you will be pulling it inwards, which is where the sideways motion of the boat is generated. When the blade is as far forward as you can get it, keep the shaft vertical and rotate your wrist the other way to angle the drive face 20° towards the stern. Then pull the blade back through the water as far as you can. At this point, quickly rotate again to push forward, maintaining enough pressure on the blade face to keep it the same distance from the boat at all times.

As you push and pull the paddle to and fro, the boat will move towards the side where you are paddle stroking. It helps to lean towards the paddle and to edge at the same time, so that the leading edge (the one nearest the paddle) of the boat is lifted. It is also possible to do this with the blade angles reversed, so that the pressure is on the outside (back) face of the paddle. The boat will then move sideways away from the paddle. This is a sculling pushover. In this case the leading edge is the one opposite to the paddle.

Sculling further forward will move the boat sideways with the bow ahead of the stern, while sculling behind will mean the tail leads. In this way, sculling can move and turn the boat at the same time.

A sculling draw. Note how the boat moves quickly sideways, creating a wave.

Sculling Draw Technique

1 Start as for a draw stroke, but with the blade only 20cm (8in) from the hull. Bend your wrists back so that the drive face is facing slightly towards the bow.

2 Move the blade forwards as far as you can reach without leaning, keeping it vertical and exactly the same distance from the side of the boat.

3 Quickly cock the wrists so that the paddle blade is pointing slightly towards the stern. (Note: the paddle is shown partly out of the water for teaching only).

4 Move the paddle back, keeping the pressure on the blade so that it stays equidistant from the hull.

5 When the paddle is as far back as is comfortable, cock the wrists back again to open the drive face towards the bow.

6 Move the paddle forwards as before, keeping the pressure on at all times. Repeat as necessary.

Stern Rudder

Sometimes it is desirable to make subtle direction changes, or to keep a kayak running in a straight line while in readiness for a turn. For this the stern rudder is extremely useful.

As the name of the stroke suggests, the paddle blade is used as a rudder at the stern of the boat. Place the paddle in the water, with the drive face towards the boat and the paddle shaft at a low angle. The back arm will probably be fairly straight. If the boat is not moving this will have no effect at all, but if you have some forward momentum the boat will probably turn slightly towards the paddle. If you move the paddle away from the hull, the turn will become more pronounced; closer to the hull and there will be less effect. If you bring it really close to the boat you may even start to turn the other way, away from the paddle.

Textbook stern rudder. The body is rotated to help place the blade as far back as possible, while the paddler looks ahead to where he is going.

A good exercise involves getting the boat up to speed, and then placing your stern rudder in the water, letting you experiment with pushing and pulling, and getting the boat to veer to and fro until it runs out of momentum, without taking the blade out of the water. This is a useful way to get used to feedback from the paddle.

A handy technique is to approach a landing place perpendicular to the shore, using a stern rudder to keep the boat pointing straight at the spot where you want to land. At the last moment, before the bow touches the bank, sweep your stern rudder forward in a reverse sweep to turn the boat 90° and kill your speed. You will finish up stationary and parallel to the shore, close enough to get out.

When deciding how to make a turn, ask yourself what you are trying to achieve apart from turning the boat. If you want to stop and turn, the reverse sweep may be better. The stern rudder does not propel you, and has little effect on speed except for interrupting your paddling.

It is possible, when paddling backwards, to do a sort of stern rudder at the bow of the boat, with the paddle placed as for the beginning of a forward sweep, the drive face pointing away from the hull. This is sometimes called a front rudder, and should be regarded as a rudder for going backwards.

TIPS

- Use a stern rudder sparingly. Think of it as a stroke to control steering, rather than to change direction.
- A stern rudder will impair forward movement, so you may prefer to use a forward sweep instead.
- Always have the drive face of the blade pointing towards the boat.
- Remember that your blade is acting as a rudder to steer the boat, and not as a brake to stop it.
- The stern rudder is used most when surfing waves, but practise it anyway, even if you don't need it just yet.

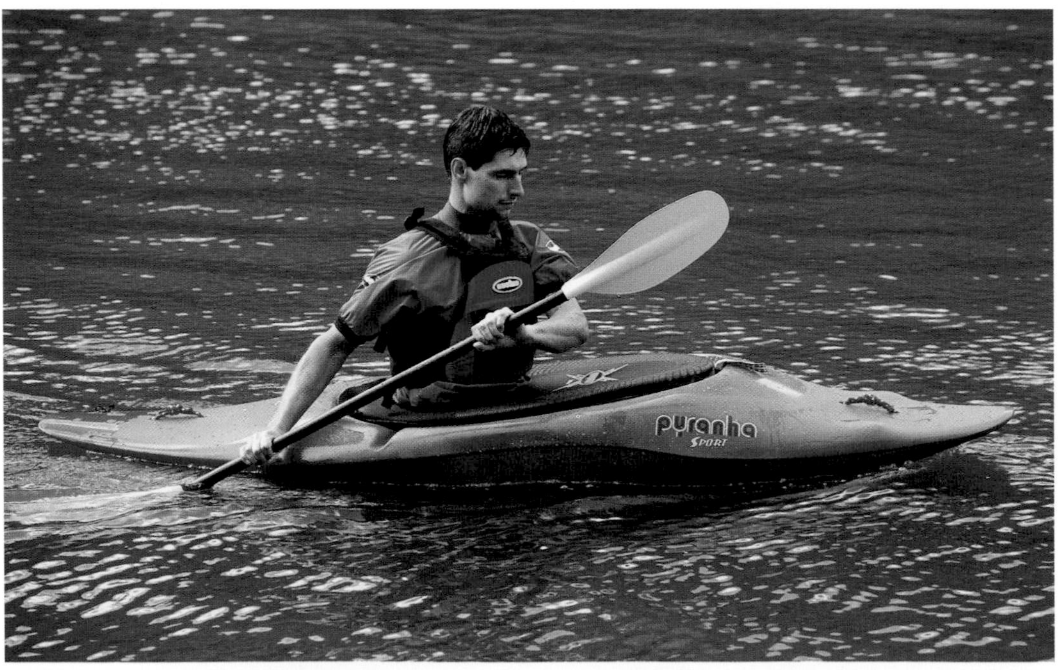

Bow Rudder

Expert paddlers seem to use bow rudders for everything, and can make complex manoeuvres while appearing just to stick in a bow rudder and lean on it. The bow rudder is in fact the fastest and most attacking turning stroke of them all, and it is the signature stroke of demanding white water paddling for this reason.

The bow rudder, unlike the stern rudder, can be a very difficult stroke to learn. It seems appropriate to mention it now, but you may find it difficult to make it work until you have mastered all the other strokes in this section. It relies on an excellent feel for what the paddle is doing in the water, as well as the draw stroke skills already covered.

The bow rudder is a compound stroke, which is to say it is a collection of smaller movements rather than one single stroke. It can make the boat spin dramatically, or it can turn the boat in a long, powerful sweep. It can be applied to great effect when the boat is turning with the current. It can also be used without any current, if you have sufficient forward speed.

While moving forwards, place the paddle vertically in the water 30cm (12in) from the side of the bow, about level with your feet, with the drive face of the blade towards the boat. Experiment with rotating your wrists to turn the blade out slightly, but resist any forces that act on the blade in the water. You will find that there is a position with the blade face almost parallel to the side of the boat when the boat does not tend to slow or turn, and you cannot feel any pressure on the blade. Roll your wrist back and turn the blade out to face the bow, and the boat will start to turn towards the paddle. The more you roll your wrist back to open out the blade, the more you will turn, but there will be a lot of force on the blade and the boat will quickly stop.

You can increase the effect by letting the pressure take the blade away from the boat, then pulling it back towards the bow in a modified draw stroke. There are many ways in which you can control the boat with the paddle blade in this mode, so experiment, noting what happens when you go with the water or oppose it.

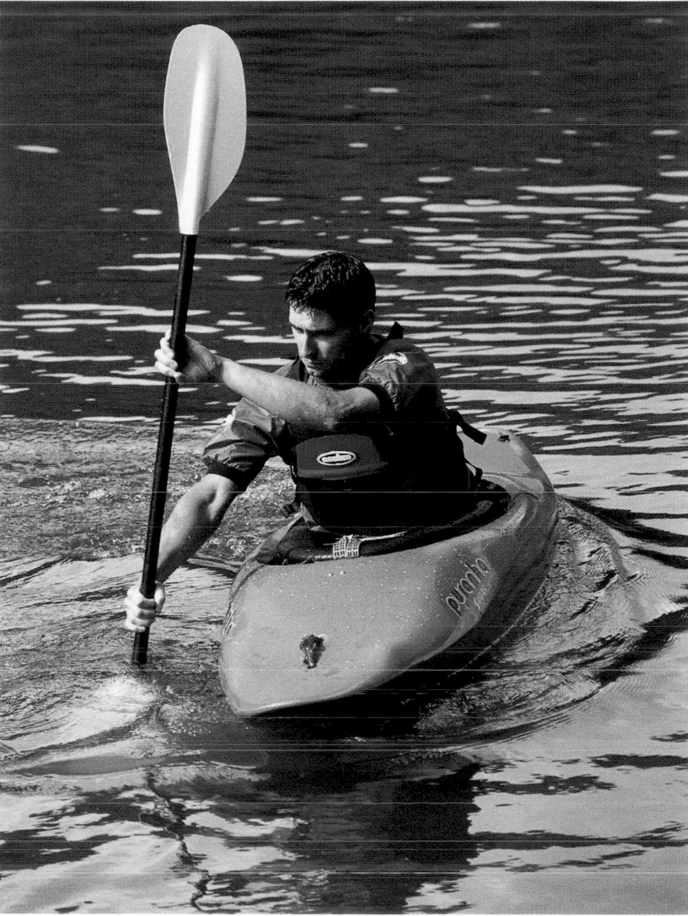

It is not easy to see how the bow rudder works by watching it. The boat can spin around the paddle up to 180° while the paddler seems only to hold his blade vertically in the water.

Don't be discouraged by your first attempts to perform the bow rudder. You will need a lot of practice to build up the strength, mobility and feel for the water that is necessary to execute the stroke properly and to make full use of it when you are paddling, and this can be very demanding on your strength and patience. But once you have it, you'll love it.

TIPS

- In manoeuvrable kayaks the bow rudder is very versatile.
- Familiarize yourself with how it feels when you rotate the blade in the water while the boat has some speed.
- Imagine running along a street and grabbing hold of a lamppost. You would swing around it, wouldn't you? This is how the bow rudder works.
- Most boats have a turning centre somewhere near your calves. Next to or slightly in front of this is where the bow rudder works best.

Low Brace

A low brace is a support stroke on the back of the blade, and it is used to keep you upright when you find yourself side-on to a wave that is trying to capsize you. All bracing or support strokes require quite a leap of faith. It is difficult to believe that you can trust your weight to your paddle blade, but this is exactly what you must do. The force that you commit to the paddle is exactly how much support you will get from it in return.

Place the blade on the surface with the drive face up. If you are moving, you must angle the leading edge up to stop it diving. It is easier to low brace with the blade behind you, but the further the blade is from the boat while flat on the surface, the better the technique will work.

Committing your weight to the blade will support you and stop you capsizing until the blade sinks too far into the water to keep it flat. If using the low brace to avoid a capsize, you must use your legs to level the craft before the paddle sinks. If the boat is moving, a low brace can be used to turn the boat, while giving some support. This is called a low brace turn.

The low brace is an important stroke that can be as useful to a white water aficionado as it is to a beginner.

The low brace is the best way to support your weight while leaning over, thereby preventing a capsize. If you are moving forwards, it will also make the boat turn towards the paddle.

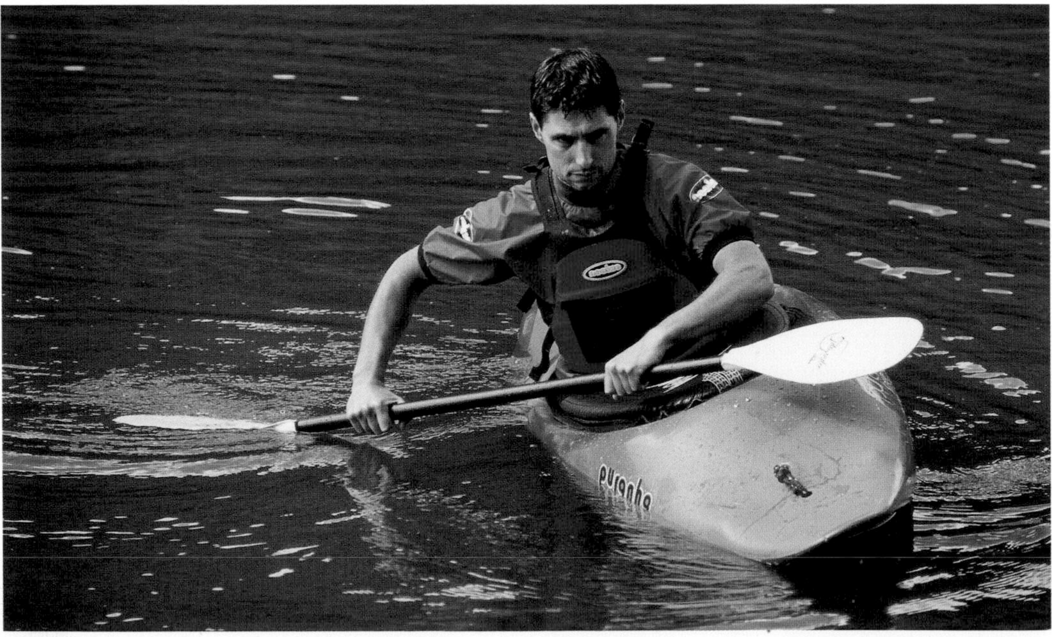

High Brace

The high brace works on the same principle as the low brace, but with the drive face of the paddle downward, and the bracing blade in the water rather than flat on the surface. This a support stroke, used to keep you upright – for instance, when a wave threatens to tip you in.

A high brace is more powerful than a low brace, and should be avoided if the latter is possible because of the huge force it exerts on the shoulders, which can lead to injury. However, as the paddle is already in the high position as you stroke, it can be more convenient to turn that stroke into a high brace when a wave is about to turn you over, rather than change your paddle position for a low brace.

Because the drive face is pointing down, high bracing demands that your elbows are below the paddle shaft. This usually means that the water is higher than the boat, either because of a wave or because you have tipped over a long way.

Keep your weight on the paddle until you can right the boat with your legs and hips. Move the weight of your body back over the boat to regain your equilibrium.

TIP

- Do not use the high brace in any powerful water feature, including river rapids. The blade may get jerked down without warning, and if the opposite arm is held too high it can be forced even higher, increasing the likelihood of a shoulder dislocation.

When taken to the extreme, the high brace over-extends the shoulders and there is a significant risk of dislocation or other, often very serious, injuries to the shoulders and upper back.

The high brace is more powerful than the low brace because you can reach further out for more leverage, and use the drive face of the paddle.

CANOEING SKILLS

Canoeing is accessible to most people because the skills for getting in and out of the boat, and having fun, are not specialized or demanding. If, however, you plan to progress to a specialist area or want to paddle longer distances, or look after friends and family while they, too, enjoy their paddling, it is time to acquire new skills.

This section outlines the basic skills and strokes that will help you use the canoe in an effortless and skilful manner. The exercises are tackled in approximately the order in which they tend to arise, although some instructors may prefer a different order.

When you are learning the following skills, choose a suitable place to practise them, and try not to progress too fast. Make sure you have mastered them before you move on. If something is not working and you do not know why, take a break and then have another go. If there is still a problem, get expert advice. Also remember that until you can do most of the strokes, you will not be able to paddle the boat to the desired location, and that is why it is vital that you know you can swim to a safe landing place.

Two paddlers charging along a flatwater river in a tandem open canoe.

Swimming with an upturned canoe after a capsize, keeping hold of the boat and paddle.

Getting into the Canoe

The first key lesson while the canoe is floating on the water is to get into the boat. It is much trickier than it looks, but it will come with practice.

It is best to start by finding a launching site where the river bank or jetty is low enough to let you step into the canoe without having to jump or climb in. Place the boat on the surface. The water should be deep enough to keep the craft afloat with your weight. If the water is deep enough to capsize in, make sure that it is deep enough for getting out of the boat when it is upside down.

Also consider how you are going to stop the canoe from floating away while you climb in. Do not be tempted to tether the boat to the bank, as this will make things difficult if you capsize. It may be possible to step into the boat while still holding on to the bank, just pick up the paddle beside you, and paddle away. Often, however, this is quite tricky. A useful technique is to place your paddle on the ground next to the boat, and keep one hand on it as you climb in. This is often easier than clinging on to a grass bank.

When the boat is afloat and you are holding on to it and the paddle, you are ready to get in. Place one foot in the bottom of the boat, and make sure it is right in the middle before you put any weight on it. Now gradually transfer all your weight on to that foot, and still holding on to the paddle if necessary, place your other foot right inside the footwell of the boat and gently sit or kneel down. Get comfortable and stable, and pick up the paddle if you have not already done so. Finally, get into your preferred sitting or kneeling position.

Getting into the Canoe

1 Put the canoe in the water close to the bank and keep hold of the nearside gunwale, so that the canoe cannot stray.

2 Make sure the canoe is floating freely, and that it won't touch the bottom when you get in. Lay the paddle across.

3 Holding on to both gunwales and the paddle, put one foot in the middle of the canoe and transfer your weight on to it.

4 When you feel confident that the canoe is balanced and stable, bring your other foot into the boat, still holding the paddle.

5 Supporting your weight on your hands, and holding on to the paddle, sit or kneel down in the bottom of the canoe.

6 Settle yourself into your preferred paddling position, still holding the paddle. You are now ready to set off.

Sitting or Kneeling?

Finding the right seating position is a fundamental part of canoeing. It is not just a matter of comfort, but a way of helping you control the craft.

You can sit on a seat in a canoe, or you can kneel in the bottom of the boat with your feet under the seat, resting your bottom against it. The latter is more stable because your weight is lower, and because you can brace your knees against the sides of the boat for better control. If you prefer to sit, find a way of bracing your legs because it is hard to balance the canoe if you are perched on the seat as if on a kitchen chair.

Kneeling correctly, with buttocks resting on the seat and knees apart.

Kneeling down and slouching is very bad posture, and provides little control.

Whether sitting or kneeling, you should always maintain good spinal posture, with your back straight. This is important for comfort, control and to prevent back pain or injury. It might seem easier to slouch at first, but this is a very bad idea.

Seating Position

The next step is called trimming the boat, which means sitting in the right position so that the boat performs well in the water. This means trying to keep the boat level or slightly bow up. A single paddler should sit in the middle, and two paddlers should sit so that the lighter paddler is in the bow.

The advantage of trimming slightly bow up is that less of the keel will be in the water, making the boat turn more easily, but you will sacrifice some speed. A level boat will be faster, but will be more difficult to turn unless it is flat-bottomed.

Sitting on the seat, with the knees against the sides, gives good control.

Sitting off-centre on the seat, or with the knees together, should be avoided.

Capsize Drill in a Canoe

If you are going to paddle a canoe it is important that you know what to do if it capsizes. The ability to swim is obviously important, but how you get out of the boat and handle yourself from there is a safety issue that should be addressed as soon as possible.

With some skill and practice you will be able to salvage almost any situation without capsizing, but sometimes it is unavoidable. When it does happen, you have a surprisingly long time to react. The question is, do you get out of the boat as it goes over, or wait until it has capsized before getting out?

If you try to get out of a canoe while it is capsizing, you run the risk of a gunwale cracking you on the head, or getting in a muddle as you try to get out. It is far better to get out once upside down, when the boat has stopped moving. Push away from the gunwale with your hands and, if possible, try to keep hold of your paddle. As soon as your head breaks surface, take hold of the boat and swim to one end. You can then either swim the boat ashore, or try to turn it over.

A reasonably athletic canoeist can often right the boat and get back in unaided. Get alongside the upturned canoe, and take hold underneath. Push it up until the gunwales are about to break the surface, keeping it level. Tread water to maintain upward force. Finally, allow yourself to sink into the water and, as you come up again, push up harder on one side than the other, flipping the canoe over with the minimum of water inside. With a really light boat it is possible to throw it into the air and land it upright. Having righted the boat, push down the side nearest to you, and reach across to the opposite gunwale to haul yourself in.

The technique for capsizing, escaping and recovering is one every canoeist should learn, but there is an advanced method that can be used to avoid the danger of being caught under the boat. When you realize a capsize is otherwise inevitable, you can jump over the side; pushing off from both gunwales as you do so ensures that the boat levels out and remains upright. Your paddle, still held in the bottom hand grip, can be used as a brake; slap it down hard on the surface as you go in, and you should be able to keep your head above water, boat in one hand, paddle in the other. This is, of course, a very safe and controlled way to exit the boat. From this position, you can swim ashore or re-enter the boat as described above.

Capsize and Get Out

1 To practise the capsize sequence, start from your usual paddling position, sitting or kneeling upright in the canoe.

2 Let go of the paddle with one hand and take hold of the gunwale of the boat.

3 Lean over to one side until the boat overbalances. Continue to keep hold of the paddle as you go over.

4 Allow the boat to capsize, still holding on to the gunwale and the paddle.

5 Wait until you are completely upside down and the boat has stopped moving.

6 Kick away from the boat and surface – ideally, still holding the boat and paddle.

Jump Out of the Boat

1 When you realize the boat is going to capsize, reach across to the lower gunwale with your opposite hand.

2 Keep hold of the paddle in your other hand and jump out. Keep holding on to the gunwale.

3 By holding the paddle blade flat you can often prevent your head from going under the water.

TIPS

- If you know the boat is going to capsize, it is worth getting out if you have enough time.
- Only jump out of the boat if you are able to do so before it flips over.
- By kicking off from the high side of the boat, you can often stop the canoe turning over.
- If you jump out before a capsize, you will be able get back in without the difficulty of righting and emptying the canoe.

Watching experienced paddlers acting out a capsize situation is a very useful exercise. All beginners should learn to capsize as soon as they first start out on the water, and most paddle club instructors make this a priority.

Go to the Front and Swim

1 Swim your way to the front of the boat, keeping hold of the canoe and the paddle if at all possible.

2 Take hold of the front of the canoe, leaving it upside down.

3 Using the paddle, if you can, and your arms and legs, swim the canoe to the shore or to other paddlers in your group.

Right Boat and Re-enter

The technique for righting the boat and climbing back in is well worth learning and practising until you are confident you can do it. The technique makes the canoeist fully self-sufficient and able to cope with almost any eventuality on the water. Once you are confident that you can do it in any reasonable weather (high winds and waves make it more difficult) you will be happy to jump out of the boat rather than to capsize, which is, in many circumstances, a much safer thing to do.

Beware, however, of becoming too reliant on your powers of self-rescue. With this technique, as with the ability to roll, there is a danger that you will simply give up and capsize or get out in a situation that may in fact have been recoverable using a decent support stroke. Obviously, you will be safer, drier and more in control if you can stay upright in your canoe.

Properly trained canoe paddlers can have great fun on white water, even when there is a risk of capsize.

Although the open canoe is in a sense more vulnerable to capsize than a kayak and is far more likely to take in water, we can see from the solutions illustrated that the canoe is just as capable a craft as the kayak, and in some ways it is more versatile. Although it is possible to re-enter a capsized kayak, it is rare to see it done successfully, and the paddler nearly always has to contend with a boat that is full of water. The canoeist can quite often avoid this. The disadvantages of the open boat are that you cannot simply roll without bailing out, unless your boat is fully kitted out with airbags or similar buoyancy (flotation), and that a canoe loaded with gear can be almost impossible to right from the water.

If there are two paddlers, or another canoeist is able to assist, then have one person hold the gunwale down on the side opposite that on which you're getting in. The trick is to hold it firmly enough so that the canoe doesn't capsize or ship any water, but not to keep the boat so level that the person trying to get in cannot pull themelves up.

TIPS

- Lift the boat slowly. The pocket of air between the hull of the boat and the water surface creates some buoyancy, which will help to support you. This shouldn't be broken until the last possible moment.
- Focus on forcefully throwing the boat upwards, not on flipping it over.
- You will need both hands to right the boat, so leave your paddle on the water between you and the canoe.
- Put your paddle into the boat as soon as the boat is righted.
- Climb into the boat carefully: to mess up this part and fall back into the water is exhausting, and you need to preserve your energy.
- If you were paddling tandem when you capsized, one of you can hold on to the far gunwale while the other climbs into the boat.
- With every capsize you bring water into the canoe: remember to bring a sponge or a small bucket next time!

Right Boat and Re-enter

1 Practise the righting sequence from any starting position in the water. Swim alongside the middle of the canoe.

2 Treading water to keep yourself afloat, take hold of both gunwales in the middle of the boat.

3 Holding the gunwales, lift the boat as high as you possibly can, then push it up and away from you so that it rights itself.

4 Keep holding the boat up out of the water as much as possible. Be prepared for your head to go under as you put all your strength into holding up the boat.

5 The boat turns over and lands right side up, with a minimum of water inside. You will have had to let go of the boat to turn it, so now get hold of the gunwale again.

6 Hold on to the nearest edge and throw all of your weight on to it. This should tip the boat towards you until you can take hold of the far gunwale.

7 Holding on to the far gunwale, haul yourself across the canoe, trying not to tip the boat so far with your weight that you take on even more water.

8 Get all of your weight across the boat, with both hands on the far gunwale. Then, bring one knee up and inside the boat. This will level out the boat.

9 Flip yourself around so that you can get into your paddling position. If your paddle has floated away, ask someone in your group to retrieve it for you.

Holding the Paddle

It may look easy, but there is a definite knack to holding a canoe paddle correctly. If you think paddling a canoe means grabbing the nearest paddle and roughly holding it, you will have no hope of mastering canoe techniques.

You can only use a paddle properly if you are holding it correctly in the first place. This is because the correct grip enables the paddler to apply the maximum amount of force with the minimum effort. It is also important to hold the paddle in exactly the same way every time you use it. This is the only way for you to become familiar with – as quickly as possible – the feel of the paddle in the water, and how to learn to interpret the feedback you get from it. This is key to becoming a good paddler.

Canoe paddles have only one blade, with a T-grip at the other end. It is important to hold this T-grip with your top hand knuckle up and thumb under, and the shaft of the paddle with the other hand. If the paddle has a curved blade, you should grip the paddle with the bottom hand so that the blade has the drive (concave) face towards you. Hold the T-grip in one hand; place the other hand so that if the paddle is held horizontal in front of you, your hands are slightly further apart than your shoulders.

Which Side to Paddle On?

Early on in your canoeing career, you are going to have to decide whether you are a leftie or a rightie – that is to say, whether you will paddle on the left-hand side of the boat or on the right. Most people are able to paddle on either side, but have a preferred side. The only way to find out is by trial and error; whether you are right- or left-handed has very little bearing on the matter.

What is certain is that whichever side you are paddling on, you should try to keep to that grip. It is the principle of canoe paddling, as opposed to kayaking, that you should be able to do everything from one side of the boat, without changing sides. Expert paddlers use cross-bow strokes to put the blade in on the opposite side from their normal paddling side without altering their grip, although some purists claim that even to put the blade in the water on the "off" side is nothing short of bad form. Ultimately, do whatever works for you, but the easiest and most stylish technique is to paddle on the on-side where possible, using a cross-bow stroke or two if necessary.

Incorrect technique. The top hand is not over the T-grip and the bottom hand is upside down.

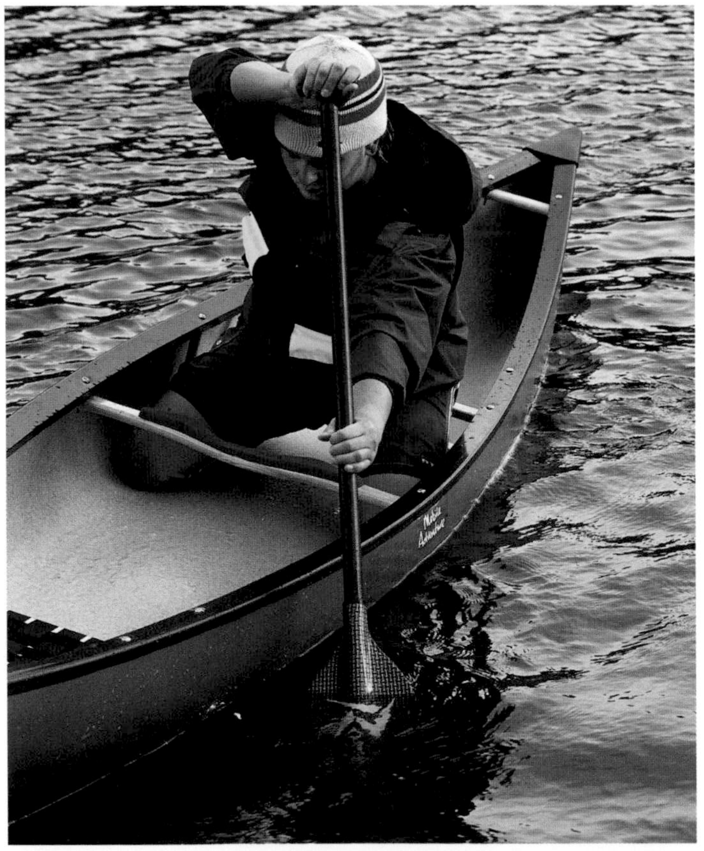

Good paddle hold. The top hand is over the T-grip, the bottom hand is above the gunwale height (thumb at the top), and the paddle shaft is vertical and close to the boat.

Using the Paddle

Beginners often find what they imagine to be the easiest tasks actually the trickiest. Using the paddle is a very good example but, by following the guidelines below, and establishing good habits from the start, you should have no problems.

For all paddle strokes you should aim to put the whole of the blade in the water, but no more. There is no advantage to the blade being deeper in the water, and it will not work properly if it is only half in. Put the blade in until it is totally immersed; keep the paddle shaft visible.

When you make a stroke, you should lean forwards to give you as much reach as possible. This also means that much of the power for the stroke will come from your leg and torso muscles, leaving your arm muscles to provide control and react to feedback from the water. It is a misconception to think that canoeing is all about using arm muscles. If your technique is good, a vigorous paddle is more likely to leave you with tired, aching legs and stomach muscles.

The next point that a canoe paddler must concentrate on is head rotation. Before making a stroke, make sure your head is facing in the direction you want to move in. So, with forward paddling, you must look straight ahead at the horizon. If you want to turn the boat to the left or right, first turn your head and shoulders to look that way. Such movements mean that the whole of your body is part of the stroke-making process. This also helps eliminate bad practices, such as looking at the blade or the end of your boat, neither of which will help your technique.

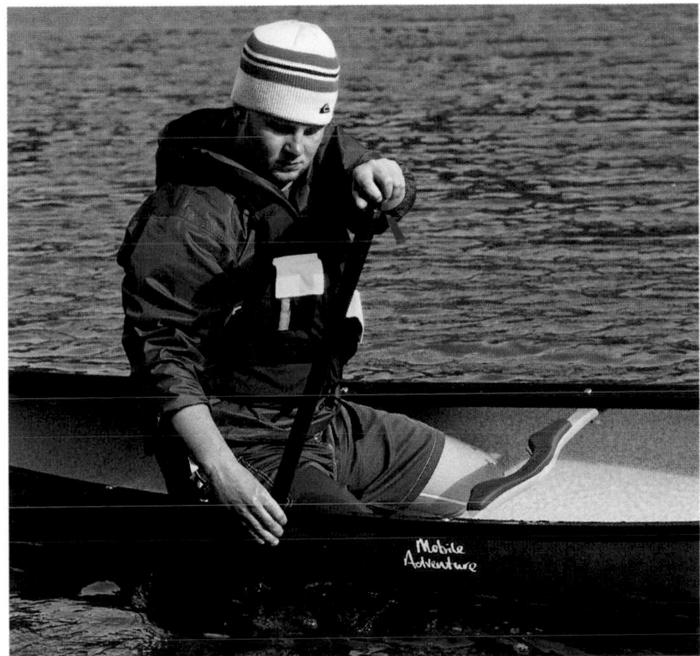

Paddling with a correctly immersed blade. The whole of the blade area is completely covered but only just, and the paddle shaft is almost vertical. The hand is well clear of the water.

Dynamic forward movement starts with good paddling technique. Holding the paddle correctly is a part of this.

Blade not fully immersed. This will not give you enough grip on the water.

Paddle too deep. Never put the shaft in the water, and certainly not your hand!

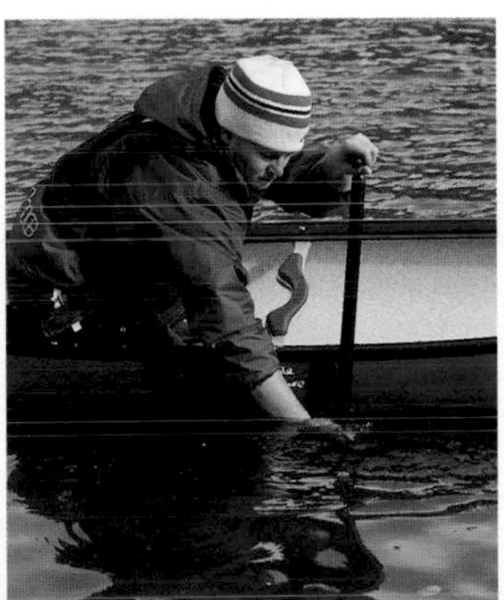

Forward Paddling

A correct forward paddling stroke is a basic requirement if you want to be a good canoeist, but it is not the easiest stroke to master. In addition to the technique for moving forwards, you will inevitably have to learn how to paddle backwards, stop and steer. Learning to combine these techniques is a useful discipline that teaches you control and the ability to respond to feedback from the water. In turn, this will help to make you a really good forward paddler.

The main aim of forward paddling is to propel the boat forwards. It is important to apply as little turning force as possible, since by turning you are making your forward stroke less effective. Normally, if you make a stroke on one side, the boat will move forwards but it will also turn away from the paddle blade that made the stroke. In order to minimize this effect, you should make the stroke as close as you can to the boat, with the paddle shaft as vertical as possible.

If you are paddling a canoe alone, you will also have to use a special technique to keep the boat in a straight line. This is called the J-stroke. If two people are paddling tandem, their paddles will be on opposite sides of the boat, and the J-stroke will not be necessary because their turning effects on opposite sides will cancel each other out.

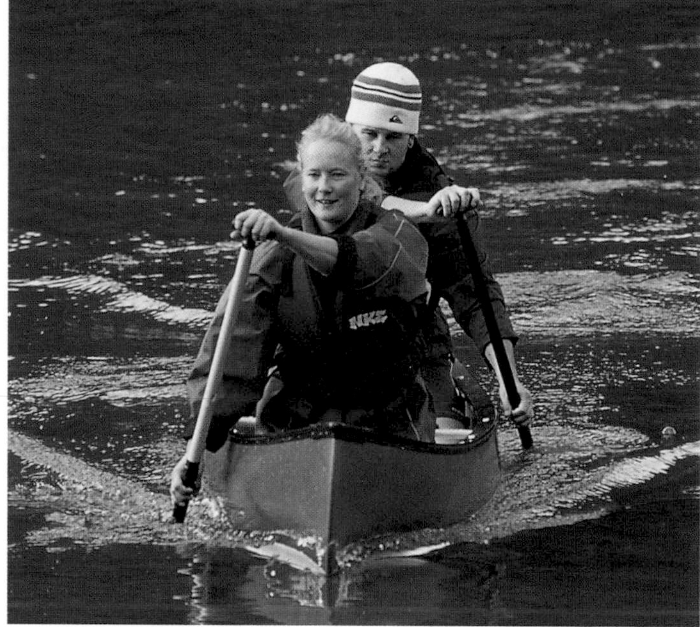

With a paddle on each side of the boat when tandem paddling, it is easy to propel the canoe in a straight line.

The lighter paddler should sit in the front of the boat when paddling tandem.

Tandem Forward Stroke

Begin with both paddlers reaching forwards as far as they can, leaning from the hips without bending the spine forwards. Both should put the blade in the water as far forward as possible, with the drive face pointing back. When the blade is fully immersed, it should be pulled back firmly, using the shoulders and torso, straightening the top arm, and keeping the T-grip on the side of the boat that the stroke is on. This will make the paddle as vertical as is comfortable.

Continue to pull the blade through the water until it is level with your seat. Try to resist the urge to pull with your bottom arm for as long as possible. When it finally does bend at the elbow, it will be to extract the blade from the water. Aim to keep the blade the same distance from the boat throughout the stroke.

As soon as the blade is out of the water, lean forwards smoothly to begin another stroke. The less time the paddle is out of the water the more control you have, but if you lunge forwards too sharply it will stop the canoe in its tracks.

Canoeists generally paddle on one side of the boat only. There is a stroke that involves reaching across to paddle on the other side, without changing grip, called cross-bow paddling, but this is usually the preserve of white water canoeists.

The J-stroke

This is the cornerstone of canoe paddling. Unless there are two people paddling the canoe on opposite sides, or you have an extremely straight-running craft, you will need this stroke to keep the boat going in a straight line.

The principle of the J-stroke is to perform a normal forward stroke but, at the end of the stroke, when the bottom arm is starting to bend, you must rotate your top hand outwards to point your thumb down. As a result, the drive face of the blade will then turn away from the hull of the canoe. This turns the stroke into a strong rudder, which arrests any turning force you may have inadvertently applied during the stroke. If you hesitate for a moment with the blade in this position, you will also be able to make fine adjustments to your course, by pushing or pulling the blade relative to the hull.

Although this may seem impossible at first, you should practise looking straight ahead in the direction of travel when making the J-stroke, rather than at the paddle itself.

It takes a while to master the J-stroke. Initially it may not seem to work, but persevere and learn to respond to the feedback from the blade. If, once you can do the J-stroke effectively, you find that some boats or conditions still make it difficult to paddle straight, there is a more powerful variation called the C-stroke. This is a J-stroke with a sharp pull of the drive face towards the hull at the very beginning, so that the blade creates a C rather than a J-shape. See the Draw Stroke for more help.

TIPS

- Practise the J-stroke for as long as it takes you to feel comfortable with it: it's key to the good handling and control of a solo canoe.
- Use the J-stroke to keep yourself in line when you are happy with your general direction.

This paddler is using a J-stroke to keep his white water open canoe on course as he moves downstream.

J-stroke Technique

1 Put the paddle in the water as far forward as possible, leaning forward to increase your reach.

2 Push with the top hand rather than pull with the bottom, and use your body as well as your arms.

3 As the blade passes your body, twist the paddle shaft so that your thumbs are pointing down. Unlike this paddler, you should aim to look straight ahead of you.

4 Keep the pressure on the paddle until the end of the stroke or else it won't work. It's a stroke with a twist, not a stroke followed by a stern rudder.

Backward Paddling and Stopping

Paddling backwards is in principle no different to going forwards, but it is a bit more difficult. Beginners will often try to change their grip on the paddle, which is a mistake – always keep the same grip.

The first thing to note is that you back-paddle using the back of the blade. There is no need to turn the paddle around because any curvature actually helps you do the back stroke. It is bad practice to change your grip. It is not possible to keep the paddle shaft as vertical as you do for forward paddling, or to keep the blade so close to the boat, but you should try to do so as much as possible. Make a big effort to rotate your shoulders as far as you can to place the blade behind you; this also gives you an opportunity to look behind you to see where you are going.

Push your paddle forwards through the water with your arms fairly straight, and make the stroke as long as you can. Most boats will turn during the stroke, so you may have to turn the back face of the blade out at the end of the stroke in a sort of reverse J-stroke, unless there are two of you paddling the canoe. Find somewhere safe where you will not crash into anything, and see how long you can keep going backwards in a straight line. It teaches you excellent control.

Don't be disappointed if you can't paddle backwards very far. It is a difficult technique to pick up, and can take a while to learn properly. Try to be as good at it as you can, but bear in mind that it is usually easier to turn the boat around and paddle forwards instead.

Stopping

Getting an open boat to stop in a straight line is almost impossible because the boat will always turn towards the paddle. If you have room to let the boat turn sideways this will be the safest way to stop. If not, stick the paddle in the water as a brake, and, when the boat turns, use a sweep or pry manoeuvring stroke to keep the boat straight. Repeat as many times as it takes until you are still. Once you have learnt the pries and bow rudder strokes, this will seem a lot easier.

Rotating the shoulders as you place the blade behind you will help you make a more effective back stroke.

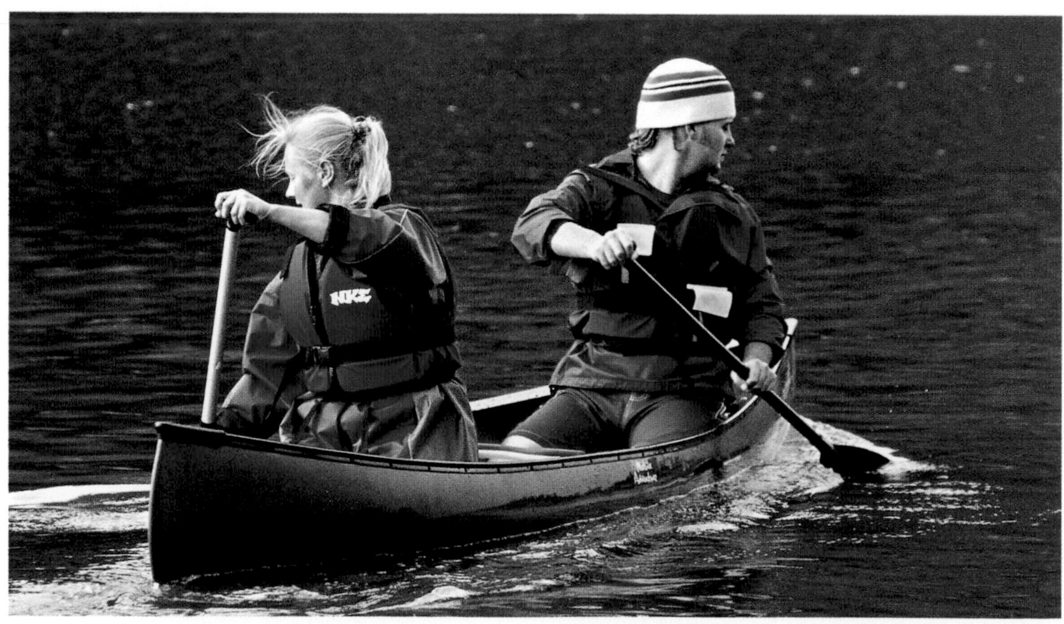

Look where you are going when paddling backwards in tandem!

Forward Sweep Stroke

The forward sweep stroke is the simplest and most useful manoeuvring stroke of all. It is used either to turn the boat on the spot, or to make adjustments to your course while moving forwards.

Unlike the technique for forward paddling, sweep strokes are intended to turn the boat as much as possible. Proceed by placing the blade as far forwards as you can, but with the shaft fairly low, and the drive face looking away from the boat. Then rotate your head and shoulders so that they are facing the direction you want to go. Now, keeping your bottom arm straight, sweep the paddle in as wide an arc as your reach allows. When you have turned enough, or the blade is close to hitting the back of the boat, lift it straight out of the water. It helps if you can edge the boat a little, using your legs, so that the side opposite your stroke is raised a little, just for the first half of the stroke.

Unlike a kayak, which can be turned through an angle of 90° or more on the spot, a canoe will only turn between 30° and 40° per stroke. It can also be used to change or correct direction while paddling forwards, by simply inserting one sweep stroke without otherwise breaking the rhythm of your strokes.

Here, the stern paddler is using a sweep stroke to change the direction of the boat on white water. The bow paddler maintains his forward stroke technique.

Forward Sweep Technique

1 Place the paddle blade as far forward as you can, with the drive face pointing away from the canoe.

2 Look over your shoulder in the direction you want to go, and sweep the blade in a long wide arc.

3 When the blade gets to the back, lift it out of the water before it gets caught and your boat trips over it.

Reverse Sweep Stroke

As the name implies, the reverse sweep stroke is the exact opposite of the forward sweep. In fact, it is a much more powerful stroke, imparting more turning force, but it should not be used while moving forwards unless to turn around and head back in the other direction, because it will effectively arrest all forward motion.

Start with the paddle blade as far back as you can reach, on the side you want to turn towards. Rotate your head and shoulders in this direction. Drop the blade into the water with the drive face towards the boat this time, and then sweep the blade forwards in the widest arc you can make, until you are pointing the way you want to go, or until the blade is about to hit the front of the boat. Lift the blade out of the water.

Again, keep your bottom arm as straight as you can throughout the stroke. It helps to lean dramatically towards the stroke because it simultaneously lifts the keel and extends your reach.

It should be very easy to turn most canoes through more than 45° with one reverse sweep. You will find that once the blade is out of the water, the canoe will continue to rotate.

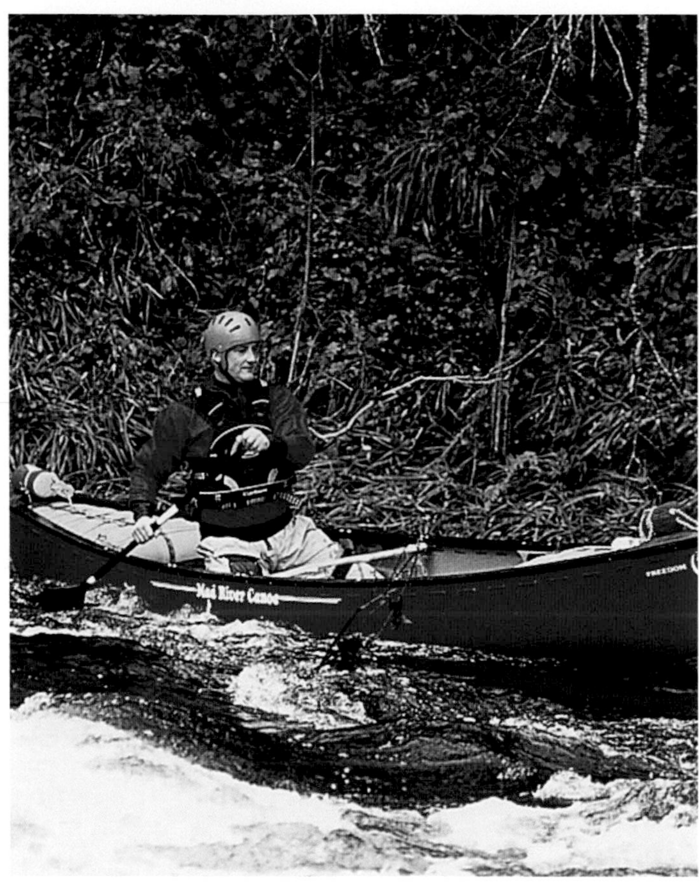

The reverse sweep is a powerful stroke. It turns the boat so well that it halts all forward progress.

Reverse Sweep Technique

1 Begin the reverse sweep stroke by leaning back and placing the paddle blade in the water near the stern. The drive face of the blade should be pointing towards the boat.

2 Lean your body towards the paddle and sweep the paddle forward in a big arc towards the front of the boat. Use your body, specifically your torso muscles, not your arms to make the stroke.

3 Continue to lean over towards the paddle, and get all of your weight behind the blade as you push it forward to make the turn. Brace your legs against the sides of the boat to help keep your balance.

Draw Stroke

Few people learn to master this way of moving the boat through the water sideways. While you can manage without being very good at it, learning to do it well helps you master many other skills.

Begin by placing the blade in the water as far from the side of the canoe as you can reach, with the drive face pointing towards the boat. Push your top arm out as far as possible so that the paddle shaft is almost vertical. Now lift the edge of the canoe, using your legs, on the side you are making the stroke, and pull the blade straight towards your body. This should pull the boat sideways about 30cm (12in) in an all-purpose boat, less in a longer boat or one with a deep keel.

Do this gently at first because, as the blade approaches the boat, you need to cock your wrist back quickly to rotate the blade through 90°, and slice it away through the water back to its starting position. If you fail to do this and the blade hits the boat, you may fall in or become unbalanced. If you try to stop the stroke before it hits the hull, the same thing will happen. That is why it is important that you give yourself the time to execute the final part of the stroke.

When the blade has sliced out of the water, and is in the starting position, you can turn your wrist so that the paddle faces the boat as before. Then repeat the stroke. If the boat tends to turn rather than move sideways, it is because the stroke is being made too far towards the front or back of the boat. If the bow turns towards the paddle, move the stroke back a little, or vice versa for the stern. It will improve your skills if you make this happen deliberately; practise doing draw strokes, alternating with the bow or stern pointing forwards.

The draw stroke, also known as a hanging draw support, is very good for giving you support in the event of a wobble or imminent capsize. When you have some purchase on the water with the blade, level the boat, and pull the boat into position beneath your body.

The technique needs to be practised over and over again, otherwise, by the time you will have thought about it, it will be too late to use it; you need to be able to use it reflexively. Being able to control your boat in three dimensions is very satisfying. Mastering these strokes will really set you on your way as a canoeist.

The draw stroke involves pulling the paddle sideways towards the boat.

Applying a twist to a bow draw can turn the boat and move it sideways.

Draw Stroke Technique

1 Reach out as far to the side as you can, with the blade facing the boat. Bend at the waist to increase your reach. Leaning the boat away from the paddle actually helps, but it is very unstable.

2 Pull the paddle firmly towards you, keeping the blade fully immersed in the water. Continue to lean the boat away from the paddle if you feel confident enough to maintain your balance.

3 Lean the boat back towards the paddle. If your body weight is not inside the boat by the time the blade gets level with the hull, you could fall into the water. Twist the blade 90° and slice away from the boat.

Stern Rudder

The stern rudder, and also the bow rudder, will change the direction of your boat. Both strokes require the boat to be moving in order to be effective.

Sometimes it is desirable to make small direction changes, or to keep a canoe going in a straight line in readiness for a turn. For this, and many of the more advanced skills, the stern rudder is a very useful stroke.

As the term implies, the paddle blade is used as a rudder at the stern of the boat. Place the paddle in the water as for the start of a reverse sweep stroke, with the drive face pointing towards the boat and the paddle shaft at a low angle. Both your arms will probably be fairly straight. If the boat is not moving this will have no effect at all, but if you have some forward momentum the boat will probably turn slightly towards the paddle.

When you move the paddle away from the hull, the turn will become more pronounced; bring it closer to the hull and there will be less effect. By pulling it in towards the boat you may even start to turn the other way, away from the paddle. If you get up to speed, and then place your stern rudder in the water, you can experiment with pushing and pulling, and get the boat to veer to and fro until it runs out of momentum, without taking the blade out of the water. You will find this a very useful way to get used to the feedback from the paddle.

A handy technique is to approach a landing place perpendicular to the shore, using a stern rudder to keep the boat pointing at the spot where you want to land. Seconds before the bow touches the bank, sweep your stern rudder forwards in a reverse sweep to turn the boat 90° and kill your speed. You will end up stationary and parallel to the shore, close enough to get out with ease.

Always think about the next strokes you need to make. When going forwards followed by a turn, use strokes such as the forward sweep that will not impede your forward motion. If trying to stop and turn, the reverse sweep may be better. Note that the stern rudder does not propel you, and has little effect on your speed except to interrupt your paddling.

The canoe needs to be moving for the stern rudder to be effective.

The stern rudder is a passive stroke that is used to correct direction and to keep the boat running straight.

Bow Rudder

The bow rudder, unlike the stern rudder, is a very difficult stroke to learn. It is appropriate to mention it now, but you may find it difficult to make it work until you have mastered all the other strokes in this section. It relies on an excellent feel for what the paddle is doing in the water, and the draw stroke skills that have already been covered. The bow rudder is only effective if the boat is already moving forwards.

Place the paddle in the water about 30cm (12in) from the side of the canoe, about level with your knees and with the drive face pointing towards the boat. Experiment, rotating your wrists to turn the blade slightly, but resist any forces that act on the blade in the water. You will find that there is a position with the blade face almost parallel to the side of the boat in which the boat does not tend to slow or turn, and you cannot feel any pressure on the blade.

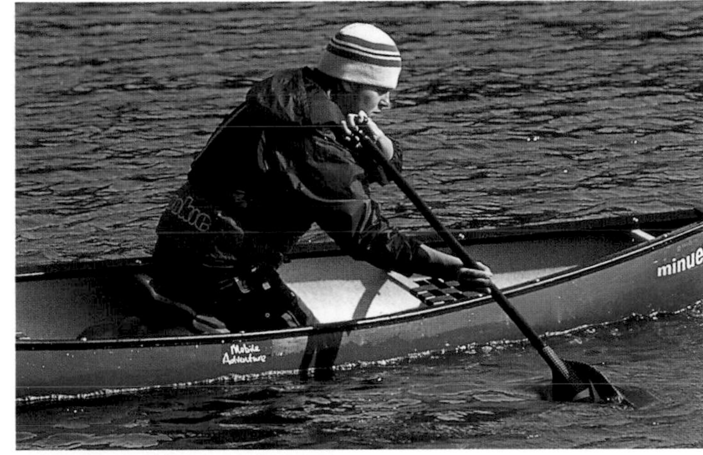

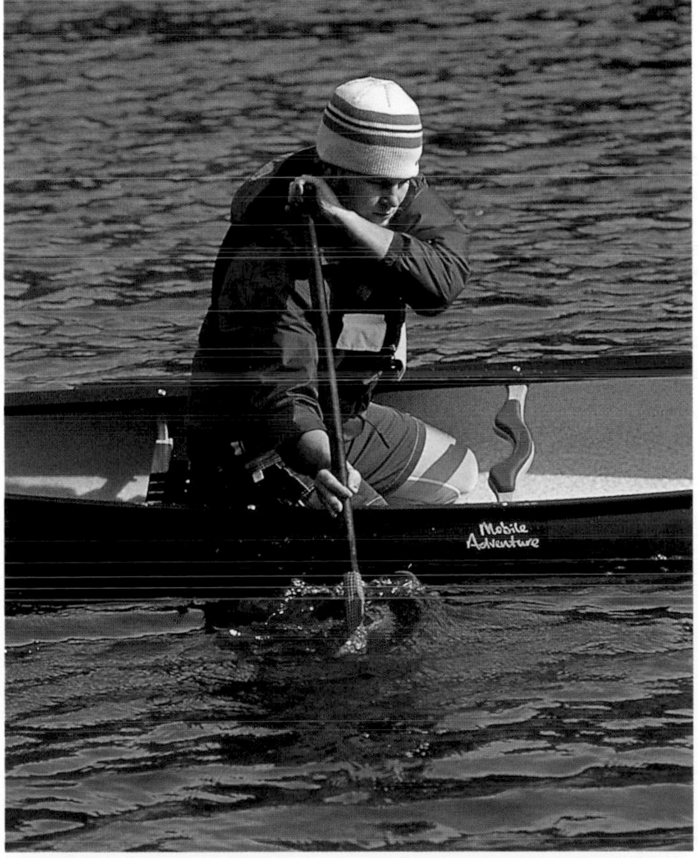

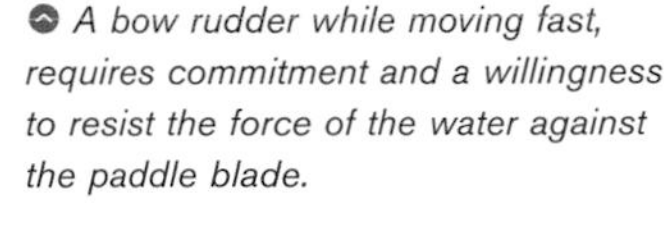
A bow rudder while moving fast, requires commitment and a willingness to resist the force of the water against the paddle blade.

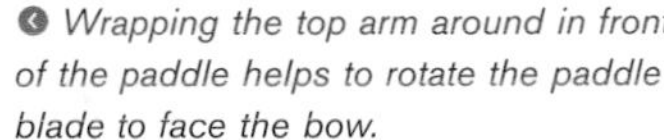
Wrapping the top arm around in front of the paddle helps to rotate the paddle blade to face the bow.

Next, turn the blade to face the bow, and the boat will start to turn towards the paddle. Bring your top hand and T-grip back until it is near your opposite shoulder. The more you roll your bottom wrist back to open out the blade, the more you will turn, but there will be a lot of force on the blade and the boat will quickly stop.

Bow Draw

You can increase the effect of the bow rudder by letting the pressure take the blade out, and then pulling it back towards the bow in a modified draw stroke. This is called a bow draw. It is a versatile canoe stroke whether you are moving or stationary. By experimenting, you will find that you can control the boat in many subtle ways, either by going with the water or by opposing it.

Sculling

The sculling strokes are refinements of the basic strokes, and will allow you much more subtle control of your boat.

Sculling Draw

The sculling draw, like the draw stroke, moves the boat sideways. It has the advantage, however, of being more useful in a confined space. For instance, when you are close to a jetty, and need to get even closer, the draw stroke may be difficult to execute. The sculling draw is also a lot less likely to tip you in.

Start with the paddle blade next to your hip, about 20cm (8in) from the boat, the shaft vertical and the drive face towards the hull. Cock your wrist back so that the blade face rotates 20° and opens out a little towards the bow.

Keep the shaft vertical and move the paddle forwards as far as you can, but keep it 20cm (8in) from the boat, and resist its tendency to slice away from the hull. If anything, you will be pulling it inwards, which is where the sideways motion of the boat is generated. When the blade gets as far forward as possible, keep the shaft vertical, rotate your wrist the other way to angle the drive face 20° towards the stern, and pull the blade back as far as you can. At this point, rotate again to push forward, maintaining enough pressure on the blade to keep it equidistant from the boat at all times.

As you move the paddle, the boat will move sideways towards the stroke. It helps to lean towards the paddle and to lift the leading edge of the boat.

You need to put the whole of the blade in the water for a sculling draw. A blade that is only half immersed just won't work at all.

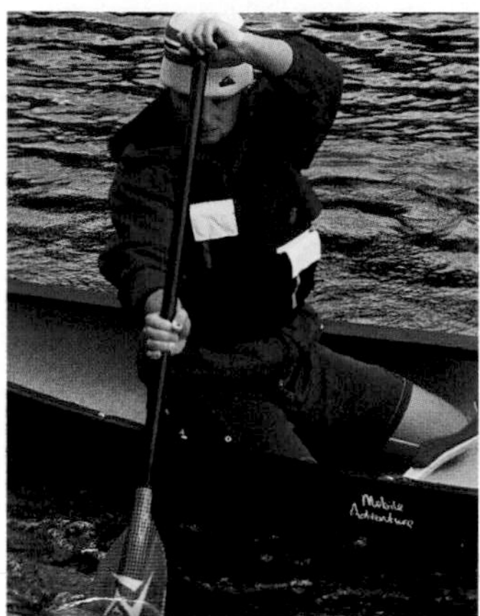

Sculling right next to your body, as here, will move the boat sideways. Sculling slightly behind you will turn the boat away from the paddle.

Sculling Draw Technique

1 With your wrist rolled back, push the blade forwards through the water.

2 Take the stroke as far forwards as is comfortable for you.

3 Now, cock your wrist the other way and bring the blade backwards.

4 Push the blade back to the start position and repeat until the boat moves sideways.

Sculling Pry

Reversing the blade angles, so that the pressure is on the outside (back) face, moves the boat sideways away from the paddle in a sculling pry. Like the sculling draw, the sculling pry exerts a continuous sideways force. Unlike the draw, the pry pushes the boat away from the blade. Sculling further forward will pull the boat bow-first in the direction of travel, while sculling further back will bring the stern around first. In this way, you can move and turn the boat at the same time.

Pry Stroke

A pry is a stroke that pushes the blade away from the canoe. It is so-called because it usually involves resting the paddle shaft against the gunwale of the boat, using it as a fulcrum or pivot as you lever the blade up and out. The basic pry is the opposite of the draw stroke, and pushes the boat through the water, away from the paddle.

Start with the blade next to the hull, the drive face in and the shaft in a vertical position. Then jam the paddle shaft against the boat and lever the blade away from you. As with the draw, when the stroke reaches the limit of its motion, you must rotate the blade 90° in order to slice it back to where it started. The sculling pry is a continuous version of the basic pry. It is used to push the boat sideways away from the paddle.

In the same way that a draw stroke can lend support, you can use a pry as a support stroke to lever the high (opposite) side of the boat down if there is going to be an imminent capsize on the side away from the paddle. This is very useful when you remember that you only paddle on one side, and you will not always capsize conveniently towards the paddle.

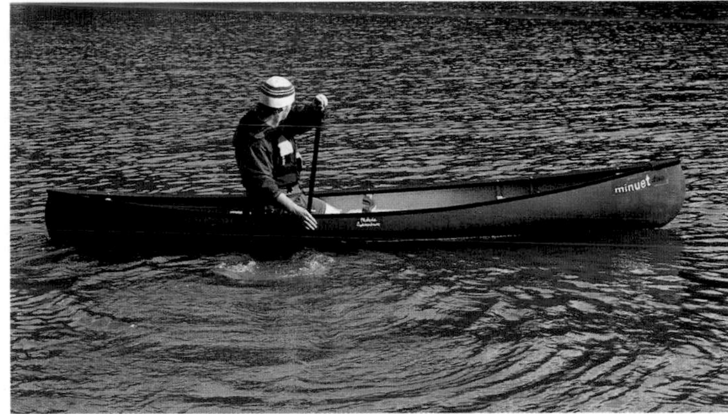

Using a pry. Although it may be difficult at first, try to look where you are going, and not at the prying blade.

Go carefully when you first start to use pries. Until you have learnt excellent edge control, using your legs and knees, there will be a tendency to overdo it and lever yourself right into the water. You need to balance the boat, so that the power of the stroke is turned into a lateral motion and not a capsizing one.

TIPS

- Proceed cautiously at first.
- Concentrate on keeping the boat level with your legs.
- Experiment with prying at different parts of the boat to get used to the turning effect.
- Look in the direction of the turn and not at the blade or you risk catching the blade on the boat.

Pry Stroke Technique

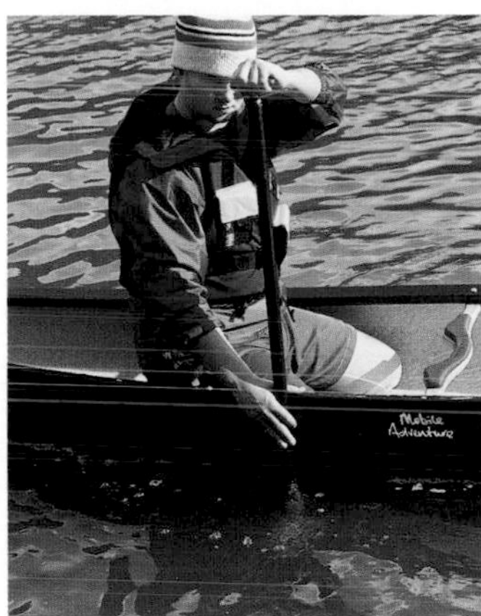

1 To begin the stroke, wedge the paddle shaft flush against the side of the boat. The blade should be just immersed in the water.

2 Lever the blade away from the boat, bracing your legs against the sides and edging the boat to keep the canoe level in the water.

3 Turn the paddle blade in the water through 90° to slice it back to the start point. Repeat until the boat has moved to face the direction you want.

Low and High Brace

The low and high brace are support or recovery strokes that are used to help you regain your balance when you are about to capsize. All support strokes require a willing suspension of disbelief. It is initially difficult to believe that you can trust most of your weight to a paddle blade, but this is exactly what you must do. The weight that you commit to the paddle is exactly how much support you will get in reaction to it.

Low Brace

The low brace gives support from the back of the blade. Place the blade on the surface with the drive face pointing up. If you are moving, angle the leading edge up slightly to stop it diving. It is usually easier to low brace with the blade just behind you, but the further it can be from the boat while staying fairly flat to the surface, the better the result.

Commit your weight to the blade and it will support you, and stop you from capsizing on that side, until the blade sinks too far into the water to keep it flat. When using the low brace to prevent a capsize, you must use your legs to level the boat before the paddle sinks, then recover the blade. If the boat is moving, a low brace can be used instead of a stern rudder to turn the boat, while also providing some support.

High Brace

This works on the same principle as the low brace, but with the drive face pointing downward. Because of this, your elbows are below the paddle shaft, which implies that the water is higher than the boat, either because of a wave or because you are in danger of capsizing. In a canoe this means that water will be entering the boat, so it is an extreme measure. The high brace is a powerful stroke, but should be avoided if a low brace is possible because of the huge force it exerts on your shoulders, which can lead to serious injury.

As with any support stroke, keep your weight on the paddle until you can right the boat with your legs, then move your body back over the boat. Don't allow the paddle to take your weight if it is above your head because you risk an injury. It is better to capsize and recover by rolling.

The canoe has tipped over until it is in danger of shipping water, and the paddler will recover using the support of the blade in a low brace.

Bracing in white water. The recovery is often so extreme that it is almost a roll.

Tandem Manoeuvres

Open canoes are ideally suited to being paddled by two or more canoeists. Tandem paddling removes a lot of the problems of steering and straight paddling. Communication is the key, however, and a constant dialogue is necessary to keep things running smoothly. Usually, the paddler at the back is in command because the back paddler can see what the front paddler is doing, and needs this information. The stern paddler will also have more effect on steering.

When forward paddling, both canoeists should paddle on opposite sides, so there is no need for J-strokes. Concentrate on keeping the strokes in time. This also applies when going back, when the stern paddler will have to look alternately over his shoulder (to check the direction) and back (to keep time with the other paddler).

A tandem turn towards the front off-side can be done while the boat is stationary or going forwards.

Turning In Tandem

1 While the canoe is moving forward, the front paddler plants a bow rudder stroke in the water.

2 As the boat turns, the rear paddler uses a forward sweep stroke to maintain the momentum of the turn.

3 The front paddler keeps leaning on the bow rudder, and can if required turn it into a bow draw.

4 The rear paddler can either finish with a stern draw stroke, or can start forward paddling again, as appropriate.

To turn a canoe in tandem, a rudder stroke at the back can be combined with a bow draw at the front to bring the boat around quickly. If turning on the spot, the front paddler can do a forward sweep and the back paddler a reverse sweep on the opposite side, or vice versa.

TIPS

- Agree who is in charge before you get into the boat: squabbling about it mid-route is guaranteed to cause you difficulties. If the bow paddler is making the turning decisions, the stern paddler should follow and complement those decisions, and vice versa.
- The strokes of a tandem pair need to complement each other. To understand the importance of each paddler's strokes, it is a useful exercise to spend some practice time swapping positions, so that both paddlers can be aware of the needs of their other half at the opposite end of the boat.

KAYAK AND CANOE ROLLING

Rolling is the art of righting a kayak or canoe unaided while still inside it. Only 20 years ago, any paddler who could complete an Eskimo roll would be regarded as an expert boater. Nowadays, rolling has become a basic skill learnt by almost everybody who goes out in a boat, even before they are very skilled at anything else.

It is possible to roll almost any canoe or kayak that you can grip well enough with your legs to ensure that you do not fall out, but clearly this skill is only of use if the boat will still be paddleable afterwards. There is little point in rolling an open boat without airbags, or a kayak without a spraydeck, because you will not be able to paddle (or indeed, balance) until you have emptied out the water.

Most paddlers learn to roll in a kayak, but there is no technical reason why you cannot learn with a single blade if canoe paddling is your one and only interest. The techniques may be quite different, but the essential principle is just the same.

An open-boat canoeist finishing a roll in turbulent white water.

Preparing to roll an open canoe. This is the typical start position for a canoe roll.

The History of the Roll

If it was not for the Inuit tribesman, who needed to right his boat without exiting to avoid swimming in icy seas, we might have had to wait a lot longer before rolling caught on.

Righting a capsized boat by rolling, without having to get out, was exclusively a kayak skill until the latter part of the twentieth century. It was invented by the Inuit tribes of sub-Arctic regions who paddled in such extremely cold seas that, had they tried to swim for safety from a capsized kayak, they would have almost certainly died. By wearing a kayaking jacket (tuvilik) of sealskin, laced on to the boat, with only hands and face exposed, the hunters could survive immersion if capsized, provided they could quickly roll up again. For this reason the skill was often called the Eskimo roll, though that term has now been abbreviated to the roll.

The first written account of rolling, by a missionary in 1765, lists about ten different techniques and drills, and is interesting because it cites a flick of the hips as the means used to right the kayak in each case. This trick is the key to effective rolling, and was overlooked by Europeans until as late as 1965.

The first non-Inuit paddler who learnt to roll was probably a curate named Pawlata, a Christian missionary to the Inuit in 1927. The Inuit had a wide variety of advanced rolling techniques that they would practise during the summer months to ensure survival in the freezing winter conditions. The skills Pawlata acquired were very basic and his technique was crude, but he took the idea of rolling back with him to Europe, and the method of kayak rolling known as the Pawlata roll is still used today as a stepping stone to more involved rolling techniques.

Rolling did not become a viable skill for white water paddling until the mid-1960s and the introduction of the more robust kayaks. Until then, spending any time upside down in white water damaged the kayak. With the advent of fibreglass craft, however, reliable rolling became the goal for any adventurous kayak paddler or decked canoeist. Before long, airbags in open boats in white water made rolling also practical for open canoeists.

Now regarded as an essential skill for anything more advanced than placid water paddling, the roll has been refined to the point that it surpasses even the skills of the Inuit. The latest innovations in boat design have led to a degree of

Rolling up in a capsized sea kayak, using the screw roll technique.

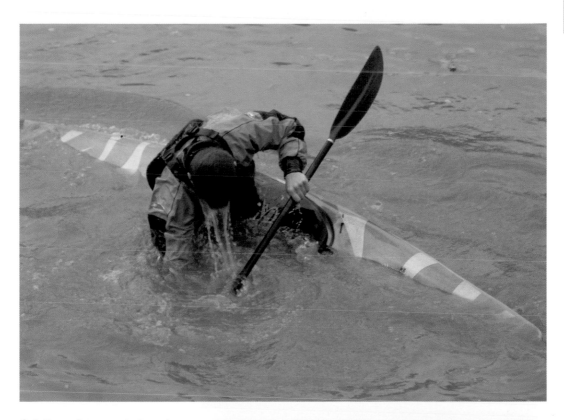

Rolling up from a capsize in an ultra-low-volume kayak. With good technique you can roll any kind of canoe or kayak.

Rolling a hi-volume general purpose kayak – notice that the head stays in the water until the boat is almost upright.

control and body fit that could barely have been imagined even a decade ago, and this has aided the development of some of the rolling skills that follow.

In the chapter that follows, we look at how to learn to roll. The hip-flick concept is constantly reiterated because it is a key element in any roll. Described thereafter are a number of different rolling styles, in roughly the order of difficulty that dictates how they should be tackled. Conspicuous by their absence are many of the "extended grip" techniques that were at one time the most usual starting point. These are not so relevant now that better rolling methods have been developed.

Learning to Roll

The indispensable, essential roll may look quite daunting, and even dangerous, but once you have grasped the basic technique, it is actually surprisingly easy.

The best place to learn to roll is in warm, clean, calm water, where a helper or instructor is able to stand waist-deep beside your boat. A swimming pool is often the best place, although repeatedly capsizing in chlorinated water may become unpleasant. If it is possible to learn in warm sea or fresh water, do so.

Unlike the majority of paddling skills, rolling is not particularly reliant on feedback from the paddle. Instead, you must master a special sequence of actions that need to be timed correctly. As with learning to juggle, each action flows on to the next. With regular practice it becomes second nature. You just think "Roll!", and you are up.

There are a few key tips of which you need to be aware before you start to practise rolling. First, successful rolling is never about heaving yourself up with the paddle. Second, the point of the exercise is to right the boat, not get your head out of the water. Third, the more of you that is in the water, the more support you will get from your natural buoyancy, so right the boat first, then let your body follow. Your head will always come out last.

Initially, your desire to breathe and perhaps your determination to succeed will make you try to get your head up out of the water. This is quite natural. Your instincts and reflexes are programmed to get your head above water at all costs. You need to stop being a human in a boat, and imagine yourself as a different creature with a hull instead of legs.

The whole principle of rolling is that, with a little support from the paddle (in the manner of a high or low brace or a sculling technique), you will be able to turn the boat up the right way using your legs. Once the boat is righted, it is a simple matter for you to sit upright and paddle away. But you must right the boat before you can afford to worry about getting your body out of the water.

There are different ways of rolling, and which one you use should be decided by your position under the water, and where your paddle has ended up. It is definitely worth trying to learn all the techniques described here, but the best roll to master first is the screw roll. This is the one roll that no paddler can do without; in fact, many paddlers don't ever learn anything else.

RULES OF ROLLING – 5 KEY TIPS

- Never try to get your body up out of the water first. Concentrate on righting the boat with your hips and legs.
- Your head should always be the last part of your body to emerge out of the water.
- Go with the flow. As a general rule, always roll up on the downstream side in moving water, or on the upwave side if you are sideways on to a wave in the surf.
- Have a sense of urgency, and roll quickly, as soon as you can. If it does not work, switch sides straight away because you are probably turning the wrong way.
- If you nearly succeed with a screw roll, it is the perfect moment to dive into a reverse screw roll the other way. The reverse screw roll is nearly always the best exit from a convoluted screw roll, but not vice versa.

When a capsize is inevitable, a paddler sets up a reverse screw roll as he tips over.

Rolling up on the downstream side. The boat is righted with the hips and legs.

As the boat rolls up, the body barely moves and the head comes out last.

Kayak Rolling Drills

The best way to become proficient at rolling is to practise the following six drills. The drills are aimed at beginners, and will take you through each stage, building your confidence and improving your technique until you are ready to attempt the screw roll, which is the one key roll that no paddler can do without.

The fundamental principle of rolling is that you can right the boat by flicking it upright with your hips. This movement is known as the hip flick, or snap, and it is the most important part of any roll. In fact, the motion really comes from the waist. If you bend rapidly to one side, your body will stay still and the boat will twist the other way. That is the secret of rolling.

It is extremely difficult to roll a boat if you do not fit it properly. If borrowing a boat, try to acquire some padding in the form of foam or a purpose-made padding kit. Make sure there is a footrest, too, because it is difficult to brace without one. And do not forget your spraydeck!

Drill 1: Familiarization

This drill helps counter confusion when you are upside down, but you will need an experienced guide to assist you. The helper should stand beside the boat in waist-deep water. You sit in your kayak, and put your hands by your sides. Then capsize, and your helper will grasp the far side of the boat and pull you upright. Do this until you feel completely comfortable, and then progress to the next stage.

(Top) An underwater view of a screw roll. The paddler bends his trunk to get his head near the surface, but he stays in the boat until it is righted.

(Above) An underwater view of a reverse screw roll. The paddler is about to start the roll by sweeping the paddle blade forwards towards the camera.

Familiarization

1 Start off sitting upright with your hands on either side of the boat. Next, capsize towards your helper.

2 Once you are upside down, the helper reaches over the boat and flips it upright. Do not try to move your arms and legs.

3 After a few attempts, you will find that you are not disorientated by flipping 360°, and can progress to drill 2.

Drill 2: Hip Flick

The next step is to hold on to the pool rail or a partner's hands or paddle for support, and practise righting the boat with the hip flick. This allows you to concentrate on the flick movement, without worrying about holding your paddle.

Practise rotating your hips from side to side, making sure that you feel quite free and will not hurt yourself. Get a good grip on whatever you are using for support, capsize and relax your arms so that they are not supporting your weight. Bend your body up towards your hands as far as possible without using your arms.

You must now try to turn the boat up the right way using your hips and legs, without trying to lift your body out of the water. Remember, no matter what else happens, keep your head in the water until the boat is upright and capable of supporting your weight.

Practise the rolling drills as often as necessary to build your confidence.

Hip Flick Practice Using the Pool Rail or Side

1 Holding on to the pool rail, position your body just under the water surface rather than hanging straight downwards.

2 Flick the boat upright with your knees and hips, leaving your head in the water. Repeat several times.

Hip Flick Practice with a Helper

1 Holding on to the hands of your helper, practise flicking the boat upright using your legs. Keep your head submerged.

2 At the end of the manoeuvre, the boat should be completely righted but your head should still be in the water, as here.

Drill 3: Using a Float

The next step is to repeat the same technique, using a swimming float or life jacket that affords much less support. This will show you whether you are really righting the boat with a hip flick from the waist, or whether you are relying too much on your arms. When you can right yourself using only a float, it is time to try rolling with a paddle.

TIPS

- Practise using whatever resources you have at your disposal on the day.
- Never practise alone: there should be someone to help in an emergency.
- If using a fixed platform, make sure you can't get stuck underneath it.
- If you are not able to practise with a swimming float you can skip drill 3, but make sure your other drills emphasize righting the boat only with the hips and legs, and not the arms.
- Do each drill perfectly ten times before you move on.
- If you are not proficient at one of the drills, go back two stages and start again from there.

Drill 4: Bow Rescue

This final confidence-building exercise is excellent rolling practice, and a useful technique when recovering from an accidental capsize if you fail to roll or lose your paddle.

First, capsize. When you are under the water, tuck your body forward into a safe position. Bang your hands on the bottom or sides of the boat to attract attention. Then push your hands up as far as possible out of the water on both sides of the boat, and sweep them forward and back to indicate that you are hoping to be rescued. A rescuer in a boat should now approach, their bow touching the side of your boat. One of your sweeping arms will make contact with the rescuer's boat. Grab it with both hands, and then use a hip flick to recover.

The bow rescue technique will save you from an uncomfortable swim in the event of a rolling mishap, which can happen to anyone from time to time.

Bow Rescue Technique

1 The paddler is capsizing and unable to roll. This is a problem situation and the paddler needs to be helped.

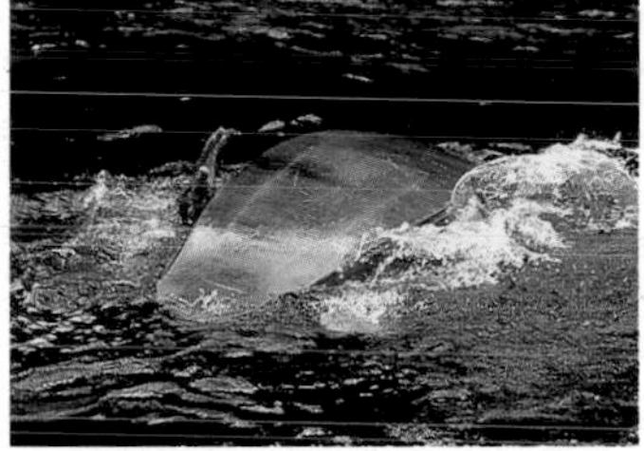

2 Upside down, the paddler bangs on the boat to attract attention, then sweeps his hands to and fro on both sides of the boat.

3 A rescuer approaches and slowly moves the bow of their boat into the path of the sweeping hands.

4 On making contact with the rescue boat, the upside-down paddler grips the bow with both hands.

5 He then uses a hip flick to right the boat, putting as little weight as possible on the rescuer's boat.

6 The paddler then sits up, ready to retrieve his paddle and continue with the trip down the river.

Drill 5: Using a Paddle with an Instructor Helping

Now it is time to try to use one of the rolls described in the following pages. Some older books suggest learning to roll with a different grip on the paddle from the one you normally have when upright. This may have some advantages, but modern boats and paddles are not really suitable. And remember, rolling relies on the hip flick concept, not on the paddle. If you cannot roll using your normal paddling style, there is something wrong with your hip flick, and there is no point in practising a bad technique masquerading as a success.

Begin by asking someone to stand in shallow water and help you, and then decide which of the rolls you are going to try. For the screw roll, which most people learn first, place the paddle in the set-up position and capsize.

The set-up position for a screw roll. This is the position you will need to get into under water, from which to start.

As you bring the paddle into position to start the roll, the helper will take hold of the blade and keep it on the surface while still allowing you to move it. You can then roll up according to your chosen method, with your helper's primary task being to ensure that you will make it if it goes wrong, and to work out whether the way you are moving the paddle is helping or hindering you. It is no use you trying to work out what you did with your paddle, because you were under the water, holding your breath, and you don't know what it is supposed to feel like anyway. An experienced helper will be able to tell you what to concentrate on. The most common problems are that the paddler is pulling on the paddle with their arms, which never works; or that the paddler is sweeping the blade correctly but the blade is angled in a way that doesn't offer much support.

Rolling with Help Using a Paddle

1 From the starting point of the set-up position, capsize with your helper standing on the other side from your paddle set-up.

2 The helper can give you a push to make sure you capsize quickly.

3 Bring the paddle into the start position. The helper takes hold of the paddle blade to add a little support.

4 Get your body as near to the surface of the water as you can without needing any support from the helper. Do not use the paddle for support.

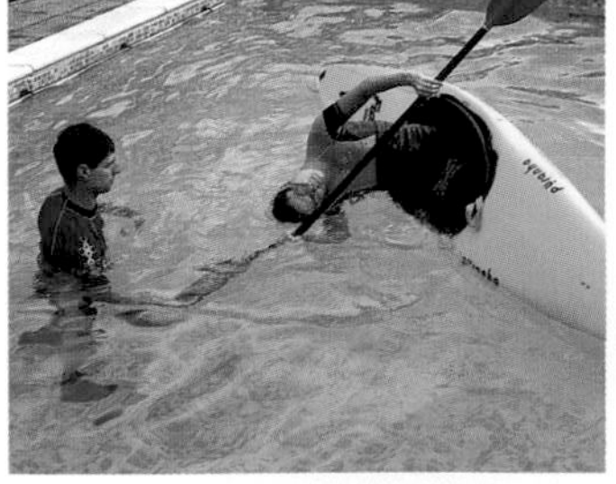

5 Start your roll from this position, with the helper holding on to the blade but providing only as much support as is absolutely necessary.

6 The helper will be ready to catch you if you fall back into the water, but with a bit of luck you will finish the roll perfectly on your own, like this.

Drill 6: Using a Paddle Unaided

This is the stage that you are aiming for on the open water, but for now you still need to have a helper standing by to flip you up if required. Do not try to visualize the whole roll but get into the correct position, and then flick the boat upright. Everything else will happen naturally. If it does not, either your set-up is not right or your hip flick is not good enough: keep practising the early drills.

> **TIPS**
>
> • Get into the start position, pause, then do the hip flick: don't think about anything else.
> • If it doesn't work at first, go back to basics and make sure you can do drills 1 to 5 in turn. Try drill 6 again.
> • Ask your helper to guide your paddle blade through the sweep.
> • If you succeed, well done, but make sure you are rolling using your body and not your paddle, or else the roll won't work when you need it.

Rolling an inflatable kayak, or "duckie", relies more on the paddle because the paddler is less secure than in a rigid kayak.

Rolling Unaided Using a Paddle

1 First you need to capsize, ready to roll on your own. You may find the capsize quite slow. Just keep the paddle close to the boat and wait.

2 Rolling up for the first time. The paddle has gone very deep without support from the helper, but the boat is coming up and the head is still in the water.

3 Completing the roll. Because the body language was good, the roll has worked despite the poor paddle action. This has been a very good first attempt.

Screw Roll

This is the most common practical roll of all. Many very proficient paddlers find they can get along using this as their only roll.

Begin the roll by placing the paddle in the water, along the side of the boat, with the water blade at the bow. The water blade is the blade in the water, used for the rolling stroke, while the other is the air blade. If you are rolling up on your right, the water blade will be the right blade. Tuck your body forward and up, facing the surface of the water on the side that the paddle is on. Next, push the air blade up out of the water as far as possible and then wrap your back arm around the hull of the boat.

This might push the water blade down below the surface, but it does not really matter. Try to keep the blade as near to the surface as possible. This starting position virtually guarantees you a good blade presentation as you roll.

Once underwater, tuck your body forwards and up, facing the surface.

Push the air blade up out of the water as far as you can.

Sweep the blade away from the boat, without pulling down on the blade. As the blade comes to the perpendicular, bend from the waist to throw your upper body into the water, and continue to sweep backwards. Continue with the bend – do not stop. You will come up leaning back, with the blade near the back of its arc.

The screw roll is very reliable because the blade gives you plenty of lift for a long time. It is also a good roll to use if you are tired. However, the set-up from which you start is time-consuming and you rarely capsize with your blades in this position. The final position is not possible in a weight-sensitive, modern short boat.

Screw Roll Technique

1 To practise the screw-roll, set up with your top arm straight and the paddle along the side of the boat like this.

2 Capsize on the paddle side of the boat. Wait until you are completely upside down and the boat has stopped moving.

3 Wrap your back arm (which is on the left here) around the boat. You should still be holding the paddle with both hands.

4 Sweep the paddle blade in a big sweeping arc across the surface of the water, reaching as far as you can.

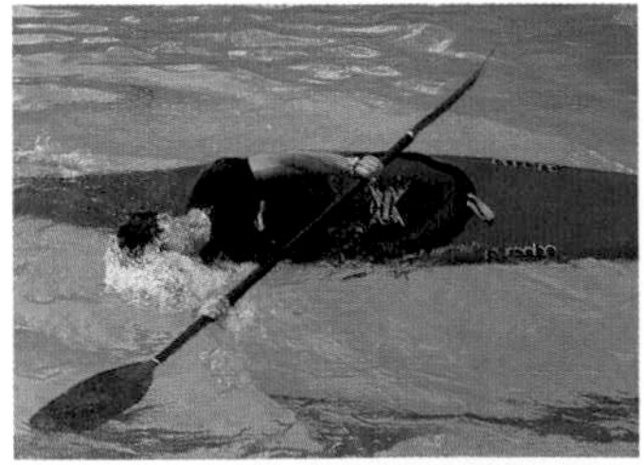

5 Arch your back to try to throw your head downwards, and right the boat with your legs only.

6 Keeping your head down in the water, continue to sweep the blade back until you are sure you are upright again.

Reverse Screw Roll

This is a favourite with freestyle paddlers and surfers because it begins on the back deck, which is where you will often end up after being hit by a big wave. Surprising as it may seem, you can still find yourself in the set-up position after falling over your blade while trying to do something dynamic.

Start by lying on your back as shown, and wrap your back (water blade) arm around in front of your face so that the paddle lies along the deck. Remember to keep your water blade to the stern and your air blade to the bow, which is the hard part of this roll. Now, capsize in that position so that you are lying face down in the water.

Next, twist your body out to that side, pushing the water blade out as far as you can, and try to get the air blade up and out of the water. Bending from the waist, use your body to sweep the water blade forward. As this happens, snap your body downwards to the right of the boat. You will have to cock your water-blade wrist back slightly to stop the blade diving during the stroke. Continue the sweep forwards, and you will emerge on the front deck, with lots of support from the paddle, which will now be beneath you.

Since you may often find yourself in the start position by accident, you may as well use this roll. It is immensely powerful if you do it correctly, and you can get away with rolling at a bad time or in a bad place. Be careful, though, because this roll exposes your face to submerged objects. From a freestyle point of view, lying on the back deck in a big water feature will either ruin your manoeuvre, give you a good thrashing, or both.

This should be the position of your paddle and body when capsized.

Reverse Screw Roll Technique

1 To practise the reverse screw, wind your arms and paddle up like this and capsize towards the paddle.

2 Use your body to sweep the water blade away from the boat.

3 It helps to wrap the air blade arm around the hull of the boat like this as you sweep the water blade.

4 Drive the water blade forward using your body, and flick the boat upright with both of your legs.

5 Bend your head and body downwards as you come back up to the surface of the water.

6 When you come out of the roll you should be leaning forward with your head tucked down. You are ready to paddle off.

Put Across Roll

Also known as the combat roll, the put across roll is far more solid than the previous two rolls, but unfortunately you really need to learn the others first. Once you've mastered all three, you'll probably find yourself using the put across (combat) roll in combination with some elements of the others, according to your circumstances.

Begin by pushing the air blade out of the water. Swing the water blade away from the boat until it's as perpendicular to the kayak as possible. Do not lean forwards or back, just bend sideways until your body is as near the surface as possible. Now, do a hip snap – hurl your upper body down into the water, and snap the boat upright with your legs. Keep your head down, face down.

If your body was bent to the left at the start, you just have to bend it as far to the right as you can, and as fast as you can. Do not do anything with the paddle except keep the drive face down, and do not move fore or aft. You will be up in a sudden snap, on a really solid brace.

It is quite hard to keep your paddle near the surface for this roll, but it does not matter. Even coming up on a vertical blade is acceptable, and often puts you in an excellent position for paddling again.

This is an exceptionally quick, powerful roll, and enables you to stay in the centre of the boat. It is good for a position in a hole, and means you are ready for another move if freestyle paddling. Since the paddle position is not critical, you can roll straightaway without having to flail around underwater. The power of the roll is especially suited to today's wide white water boats, in which you need to do the roll quickly or you will not succeed. You do need quite a bit of sideways flexibility, but with practice that is achievable.

You can modify this freestyle roll to make it a super combat roll. Just lean ridiculously far forwards, so that your nose is on the deck. Keep your arms and paddle forward, too, and do the roll across the front deck without sitting up until you are upright. It is more of an upper body snap than a hip flick, but if you can do the freestyle version you will not find it hard to master this one. It is nearly as powerful, and protects your face from any impact in shallow water.

If you are in a position to start a screw roll, the combat roll is just the same without the sweeping of the paddle, and with the body modified to move across the boat only. If, on the other hand, you are on the back deck, as for a reverse screw roll (this is much more common), then you can begin as for a reverse screw and convert to a put across roll as you get the paddle to the perpendicular.

Put Across (Combat) Roll Technique

1 Begin from the same set-up position as for a screw roll. Capsize with the paddle along the side of the boat.

2 When you are completely upside down and the boat has stopped moving, push the paddle up above the water.

3 Bend your body up sideways, so that you are as near to the surface as you possibly can be.

4 Plant the paddle so that the drive face is pointing down, then bend your body aggressively down on the other side.

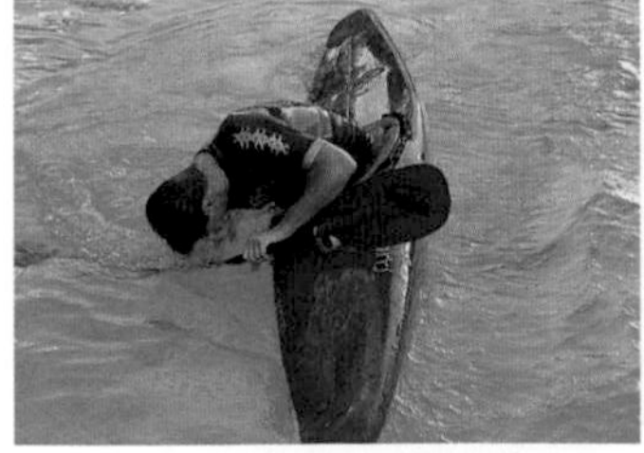

5 Concentrate on levelling the boat by bracing your legs. Your head will come out of the water as the boat levels off.

6 Finish upright, and keep both your hands on the paddle if you are not practising in a swimming pool.

Hand Rolling

The following rolls are quite sophisticated, and can only be approached when you have acquired all the preceding skills.

The front and back deck hand rolls have a variety of benefits, the main one being that they will hone and fine-tune your paddling skills for more advanced future techniques. Hand rolls are a useful and advanced skill. Many instructors would claim that you should never have to use a hand roll, but it can save you a long and unpleasant swim if you are unfortunate enough to drop your paddle.

Furthermore, it is an excellent training exercise to ensure that your roll is not over-reliant on the paddle. This is a weakness in many people's rolling technique, and can mean that when tired or in very turbulent water their roll will fail them just when they need it most. It is a good idea, therefore, to work on a solid hand roll in both the forms described here, thereby improving your technique for the main types of paddle rolls.

The best way to learn to hand roll is to build up to using less and less support. In the same way that you built up the six drills when you first learnt to roll, practise initially by holding on to the pool rail or a partner's hands, focusing on putting less and less weight on the hands and righting the boat just with your hips. Then try with a flotation device in your hands, and after that, a swimming float, until you can right yourself with your only support being your cupped hands in the water.

Back Deck Hand Roll

This is the easiest way to hand roll. Lean back and out to the side as you would for a reverse screw roll, and reach out to the same side with both hands, palms facing downwards. Bend up to the surface as much as you can. When you are fully extended in this position, sweep your hands downwards to lend support, and simultaneously hip flick as hard as you can. Arch your body back as you do so, keeping your centre of gravity as near to the boat as you can. Since your top arm will not be able to remain in the water for the whole move, throw it across to the other side as you come up, and this will help balance the boat in the slightly tenuous finish position.

The back deck hand roll is easier to perform in many boats than the front deck variant, mainly because lying on the back deck gives you such a low centre of gravity. It is possible to succeed even if you are quite lazy about it. However, as with the screw roll, the finish position of the back deck hand roll is rather unstable, and the slightly more difficult front deck hand roll will be much more practical in a genuine emergency situation.

Back Deck Hand Roll Technique

1 Start the manoeuvre by capsizing into the water, leaning back a little, with your body leaning to one side.

2 Keep your body turned to face the water as you go over.

3 Maintaining this position under the water, reach out to the side with your cupped hands.

4 Sweep your hands downwards and keep them together, and use hip rotation to right the boat.

5 Arch your back and throw your top arm across the boat for balance as the boat rights itself.

6 Finish the roll by leaning back on the deck, with a hand in the water on each side of the kayak.

Front Deck Hand Roll

This very useful hand roll relies on the hip flick, mobility and timing. It utilizes the technique used for the put across roll.

Bend up to the side to bring your head as close to the surface as possible, but do not lean back. Rotate your upper body so that you are facing downwards. Reach out to the side as far away from the boat as you can, hands cupped and palms down. Then sweep the hands down into the water using your torso as well as your arms, and hip flick aggressively. This time you will come up with both hands still in the water on the same side of the boat, but it may help to switch one hand across right at the end to help you keep your balance.

With this and the back deck hand roll, even more than rolling with your paddle, it is essential that your head stays in the water until the roll is effectively finished. This demands commitment and a good level of flexibility, but the roll will never work if you have to support the weight of your upper body as it gets out of the water – your hands simply do not provide enough lift.

It is fairly easy to hand roll narrow boats such as those used for slalom and polo, and some fast sea kayaks. However, the modern general-purpose kayak is wide and flat-bottomed, and is generally hard to right only using your hands. It is best, therefore, to learn in a pool using an easy boat such as the polo kayak.

With either the front or back deck hand rolls, you will find that the more complex hand movement is better than slamming the hands straight down. Imagine that you were swimming in a "doggy paddle" style: this helps you to reach out further and sweep a more efficient arc. In addition, if one hand paddles slightly after the other, this extends the amount of time that you have support during the roll. Try sweeping the top arm first, which makes sense, since as you roll up the top arm won't be able to reach the water. Alternatively, you can try sweeping the bottom arm first and getting in three strokes with your hands (bottom, top, bottom). Remember to hip flick as soon as the first stroke gets a hold of the water.

Underwater shot of the start position for the front and back deck hand rolls.

Front Deck Hand Roll Technique

1 Start the maneouvre by turning your whole body to one side of the boat to face the water and capsizing.

2 As soon as you are underwater, you need to reach out as far as you can away from the boat.

3 Sweep both your hands downwards and hip flick hard to rotate the boat.

4 Keep both your hands moving downwards and continue the hip flick for as long as you can.

5 Drop your head forward on to the spraydeck (spray skirt).

6 Complete the roll with your head and body tucked forward, as shown. Your arms should be wrapped around the boat.

Canoe Rolling

The technique for rolling a decked canoe would be essentially the same as for a kayak, but using a canoe paddle means you can only use the normal rolls on one side. Many canoe paddlers change their grip if they need to roll on the other side, but this has several disadvantages, especially in turbulent water. It would be very easy to lose the paddle, and a better solution is to learn a cross-bow roll. In this roll you flip over the paddle blade in mid-roll to keep it flat on the water, a useful skill that eradicates much of the vulnerability of canoe paddling. If you are learning to roll an open boat, some of the positions are a little different because it is not possible to reach over the hull of the boat. It is also difficult to finish the roll because the boat is very wide and unstable when it is on its side.

Underwater view of the start position for a canoe roll.

Rolling up: the canoe is on its side but the paddler's body is underwater.

Most open canoe paddlers use a roll that is somewhere between a reverse screw roll and a put across roll, because to finish leaning forwards is a more tenable position in an open boat. If you are paddling a decked canoe, any kayak roll would be suitable. Once you are confident rolling on your "on" side, start experimenting with a cross-bow roll. Visualize the start and finish positions. You will have to flip the blade over at some point, or you'll get twisted up!

Canoe Rolling Technique

1 You can set up for a canoe roll with the paddle straight in front of you. Lay the blade of the paddle flat on the deck.

2 Capsize your boat and reach out to one side with your paddle. Extend the paddle as far as you can.

3 Use hip rotation to roll the boat upright. Keep the paddle extended as you roll the boat towards the surface.

4 Press down in the water with the paddle and lean forward as your body comes up out of the water.

5 Tuck your head down low and keep holding the paddle in the water in this rather unstable final part of the roll.

6 When you finish the roll you should be upright, with the paddle in your hand. You are ready to paddle off.

T·Y·F

KEEPING SAFE

Safety and Rescue

While good planning and appropriate equipment can and will prevent many difficulties, accidents still happen. This section is intended to make you aware of some of the issues, so that you will always be prepared. More detailed advice on the correct equipment is found in other sections of this book, but you should be aware at all times that the right gear for the job is an important contributing factor to safety in any situation.

Practise the following techniques to a proficient level, and make sure that you know how to use any equipment at your disposal. Otherwise it'll just waste your time and get in the way just when every second counts and you need to get it right.

Communication

The biggest part of safety and rescue on the water is communication. Make sure you know your own, and your paddling group's, level of ability and experience. Keep a regular dialogue going as much as is possible, so that everyone is aware of each other. If something goes wrong, keep communicating. This is important to enable the most experienced/able on hand to take the right action, and to reassure the victim. People start to feel isolated and scared very quickly when something is wrong and no-one is talking to them.

▲ Talking through the plans for the trip in advance can eliminate confusion later.

▼ To ensure basic safety, there should always be a minimum of three people involved in any paddling trip. Good communications will head off most of the potential problems.

A shoulder belay is one way to pull a swimmer or boat from the water.

These two have capsized their sit-on kayak, but by keeping hold of it they ensure they don't get tired or separated.

Capsize Drill

How to do it is covered in detail on pages 58 and 78. Everyone going canoeing or kayaking should be confident that they are capable of competently exiting the boat in the event of a total capsize. If you don't think someone is safe to do this, you should say something. It is fairly common to capsize even in calm water, and whether someone can get out of the boat when it happens is not something that should be left to chance.

Boat to Boat Rescues

It is often possible to swim or wade to safety after a capsize, with no harm done. If, however, you are in deep water or far from shore, it is handy to have practised some of the boat-to-boat rescue techniques described in detail on page 32. With the exception of sit-on-tops, which you can right and climb straight back on board, most kayaks will need to be emptied by another paddler before you can get back in. See page 33 for more details of how to do this. Canoes can be self-rescued more easily, if you have practised the trick in advance.

Towing

Sometimes, whether because of injury, tiredness, or broken equipment, it is necessary to undertake the towing of another paddler or their boat. You can use a variety of different methods, whether boat to boat, or using a specialist waist towline, or just a webbing sling over your shoulder. The most important consideration is to ensure that in the event of a capsize, neither the tower nor the towed is putting themselves in more danger than they were in before the rescue was undertaken.

SAFETY RULES

- Always wear a flotation aid, and put it on before you get into the boat.
- Learn how to capsize as a priority.
- It is more important to rescue the victim than the boat.
- Never undertake a rescue that puts you or the victim in more danger than you were already in.
- Only ever practise rescue procedures in a safe environment.

Most countries have an Air Sea Rescue service that will come to the help of paddlers in trouble at sea.

Medical Knowledge for Paddlers

Kayaking and canoeing are very safe sports when compared to most other adventure activities, and much safer than team contact sports such as football, basketball, rugby or cricket. However, minor injuries are commonplace in all sports, and in addition to knowing how to cope with them, you must also be aware of problems that are specific to paddlers.

The skills required to tackle serious and/or life-threatening injuries in a remote environment cannot be learnt from a book. If you intend to paddle in situations where such threats are possible, it is vital that you go on a registered first-aid course to practise the techniques involved.

Of the few injuries that do occur, most happen while actually paddling, and not while capsizing, rolling or swimming.

The most common mechanism of serious injury is striking an object such as a rock, paddle or another kayak. The next most common are traumatic stress injuries caused by the impact of water against the body or equipment, and overuse injuries such as tendon problems, particularly in the wrists, and chronic back problems.

Rolling up with the head tucked on to the front deck can save you from knocks to the head and facial injuries.

A bivvy bag can be used to retain heat and prevent wind chill. Note here the buoyancy aid being used as a pillow to stabilize the head position and maintain clear airways.

Minor Cuts and Bruises

Cuts, bruises and splinters are far more likely than fractured limbs. Immersion of the affected area in cold water and/or wind chill ensures that minor cuts and bruises will not usually become painful until you get off the water. If there is an open wound, however small, be aware that it might get infected and decide whether to close or cover the wound before the wound gets wet, if you still have a choice. Clean water (fresh or sea), should be used to clean the wound, and this will temper any pain. If you suspect the water is dirty, keep the wound dry.

Hypothermia

If you become excessively cold you will slowly succumb to hypothermia unless you are able to warm up your body. The victim is unlikely to realize it themselves, but early symptoms may be noticed by other paddlers. These include:

- Irrational behaviour.
- Loss of co-ordination.
- Loss of communication skills.
- Memory lapse.
- Loss of motivation and will to move.

Hypothermia can be caused by sudden cooling, for example taking a swim in cold water, or by slow progressive cooling through the onset of exhaustion and/or inadequate insulation over a period of hours. The cause might even be a combination of the two. With the former, it is correct to warm up the victim quickly, when back on land, using a warm bath or shower, or switch on the car heater.

In the case of profound hypothermia caused by slow heat loss, this would be ineffective, extremely dangerous and could result in heart failure. Instead, get the victim dry and insulate them as much as possible with clothing, a hat, gloves, sleeping bag or anything else to hand. If you are carrying a bivvy bag as part of your first aid kit, you can put the victim into it. If necessary, you can get into the bivvy bag with them to increase the temperature. Check constantly that their air passage is clear, and get professional medical help as quickly as possible. The victim will not be able to do anything to help himself.

Remember that prevention is better than cure. If you or anyone in your paddling group is exhibiting the normal signs of getting cold, for example shivering, and loss of feeling in the extremities, while on the water, act immediately before hypothermia can set in. Get the person away from the water, and get them warm.

Hyperthermia

The opposite of hypothermia is heatstroke, also known as hyperthermia. The symptoms are loss of colour, a high temperature but not necessarily sweating, and shallow breathing. The victim will feel faint and nauseous. Cool down the casualty gently by moving them into the shade and giving them lots of cool fluids.

By far the most common cause of hyperthermia in paddlers is moving around off the water when it is hot, while still wearing all the insulation that was intended for the colder conditions on the water. The best immediate treatment is to remove as many levels of clothing as necessary to enable them to cool down before they overheat.

Shock

Traumatic injury or a frightening experience can lead to shock. Similar symptoms to those of hypothermia occur. The victim may be disorientated and not capable of looking after themselves. Shock can be treated as follows:

- Treat the cause if it is physical.
- Make the victim comfortable, and place them in the recovery position if possible.
- Keep the victim warm, and provide warm drinks if there is no reason to preclude this (if the victim is unconscious or has a head or facial injury).
- Watch the victim constantly in case they stop breathing or fall in the water.
- Provide professional medical attention as soon as possible.

EMERGENCY ACTION

A realistic attitude towards personal safety on the water is essential, and a few common sense precautions will ensure you are as prepared as you can be for an emergency. Attending a registered first-aid course will give you confidence in your ability to react swiftly, and can help save lives. Contact your local kayak or canoe club for details of appropriate courses in your area.

- Drowning poses an ever-present threat to paddlers of all levels and on all types of water. Knowing how to treat a drowning person can mean the difference between life and death. First aid treatment for drowning always begins with cardiopulmonary resuscitation, and while it is beyond the scope of this book to teach this, it is recommended that you attend a first-aid course to learn what to do. The threat of drowning can be minimized by following three basic rules:
    1. The ability to swim 50m (170ft) in light clothing.
    2. Personal flotation aids should be worn at all times.
    3. A minimum number of three people in any paddling group.
- Anyone who is unconscious or semi-conscious must be placed in the recovery position to ensure that their breathing remains unobstructed. Make sure your first-aid training includes the recovery position.
- If you need to telephone the rescue services for help, find out your exact location before you call so that they know where to look for you. Include an up-to-date 1:50,000 map and a compass as part of your safety equipment, as well as a torch to help you read it if the light is poor, and give accurate map co-ordinates for where you are when you make the call.
- Keep your first-aid training up to date, and practise safety and rescue procedures with your group on a regular basis. Practising in conditions where the emergency is likely to happen – such as on a river bank in wet and windy weather – is particularly useful.

Head Injuries

These can be caused by anything from low-hanging tree branches to rocks in the water when you capsize. Anyone suffering a severe blow to the head or who becomes unconscious for any reason needs professional medical advice as quickly as possible. If this happens when the group is out on the water, return the victim to the shore, and put them in the recovery position until help arrives. Do not move the victim unless it is absolutely essential.

Improvise an effective stretcher using two kayak paddles and flotation aids.

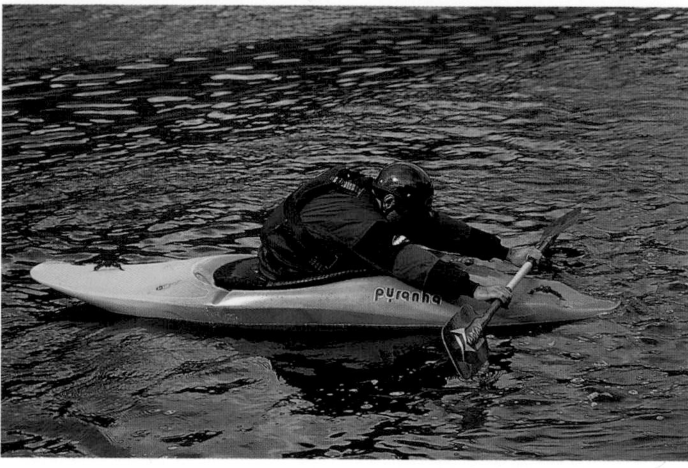

Warming up and stretching thoroughly before paddling is a good way to prevent injury and mishap on the water.

Cramp

Cramp is a painful muscle spasm that occurs when the blood supply to the affected area is impaired. It commonly affects paddlers because of their sitting or kneeling position, especially in cold weather conditions.

The condition is not serious but the pain can be severe. The best treatment is to try to stretch the muscle, counteracting its contraction, and to massage the whole area to improve the circulation. Cramp can occur in any muscle but it is particularly common for boaters to get it in the calves and the feet.

Cold Hands

Paddling in very cold water can cause extreme discomfort in the hands and particularly in the fingers. Unfortunately, the instinct to stop and warm up the hands can prolong the time you are on the water and the discomfort. A good solution is to carry on paddling and getting wet, ignoring the fact that your fingers are getting cold, until they really begin to hurt. If, at this point, you continue to exercise quite hard, you can provoke a reaction from your blood vessels which, though initially painful, will after a few minutes stop the discomfort. You will then be able to use your hands normally and can continue paddling.

A group of kayakers venturing out to sea with a qualified instructor.

Surfer's Ear

Surfer's ear, also known as exostoses, is an increasingly common complaint among paddlers who regularly get completely wet. The complaint is the growth of bony lumps in the inner ear as a result of the ear canal being constantly exposed to cold water and wind chill. After several years of regular exposure, the lumps can impair the hearing, and will cause constant ear infections by preventing the inner ear from drying out as quickly as it normally would. The best preventative measure is to protect the ears whenever you paddle by wearing a skull cap or earplugs. These are available from most paddling suppliers. Consult your doctor if you suspect you might have surfer's ear.

Shoulder Dislocation

One of the most common traumatic injuries experienced by canoeists and kayakers is shoulder dislocation, and in particular anterior dislocation (where the upper arm is forced up and back beyond its normal range of movement until the shoulder joint is dislocated). In rare cases the joint is able to relocate on its own, but more usually it will have to be repositioned by an expert medical practitioner. The injury is extremely painful, precluding further activity of any sort, and usually requiring evacuation. All you can do is to try to stabilize the injury to prevent further pain and damage. It usually takes months to rehabilitate from a dislocation, so prevention is the way to go. Avoid high bracing, reaching too far behind you, and paddling without first warming up.

FIRST AID KITS

Always carry a basic first aid kit and include the following items. Look through the equipment in your kit, and make sure you know how to use it. Better still, attend a first aid course so that you can practise the theory.

- First aid manual.
- Sterile bandages.
- Sterile plasters.
- Sterile gauze and burn patches.
- Mild relief tablets for headaches, nausea, and bacterial infection.
- Surgical tape.
- Scissors and tweezers.
- Thermometer.

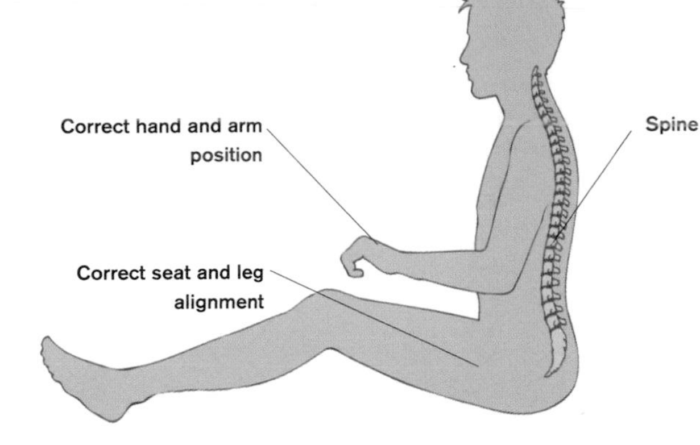

Tendonitis

Paddlers are prone to tendon problems, particularly in the wrists and elbows. This tends to be a chronic (ongoing) complaint, which can best be addressed by using paddles with low angles of feather, and simply not overdoing it. Gripping the paddle too tightly when anxious can exacerbate the problem, as can paddling aggressively with a poor or jerky technique.

Back Pain

Back pain is common for kayakers and canoeists alike. Back problems can be minimized by good all-round training, warm-up and stretching routines, but you must also maintain a good body posture.

The spine needs to maintain a correct curvature, with particular attention given to the curve in the lower back. A kneeling canoeist can more easily maintain this posture while paddling, while a kayaker will find it almost impossible. Failure to maintain correct lower back posture while working hard can result in severe back pain. The problem is compounded if you get into a car without adequate lumbar support to drive home. Lying in the bath at home will further aggravate the condition: unless you can lie completely flat and float, the shape of the bath will bend your spine in all the wrong places.

Perfect posture, with the spine in the shape of a letter S, reduces pressure on the invertebral discs in the lower back.

Perfect Posture

All back pain should first be tackled by checking the posture. Perfect posture is the position of the seated spine when there is the least amount of pressure on the intervertebral discs in the lower back. Every spine has it own unique shape. When this shape is preserved the posture is perfect. However, the human spine is a vertical flexible column that was not designed to be seated. Perfect posture is nearly impossible to attain for long periods: it must be supported. Holding the spine in the shape of a letter S when kneeling, sitting or standing will support the spine and maintain perfect posture.

A dislocated shoulder or arm injury can be stabilized very effectively using a flotation aid in this manner.

An awkward capsize can easily lead to injury if there are any rocks or boulders beneath the water surface.

Glossary

Aft Toward the rear of the boat.

Asymmetric A type of paddle on which the top side of the blade is longer than the bottom side.

Beam The width of the boat.

Blade The part of the paddle you put in the water; can be used as a word to describe the whole paddle.

Boater Common generic term for a canoeist or kayaker.

Bow The forward-most part of a boat.

Bow draw A stroke that pulls the bow of the boat sideways through the water.

Bow paddler The paddler in the forward position.

Bow rudder An advanced steering stroke that is used to turn the boat quickly while it is moving forwards.

Break-in Enter the current from an area of slack water.

Break-out To exit the current into an area of slack water.

Buoyancy aid A vest or jacket designed to give added buoyancy to a swimmer, but not buoyant enough to hinder swimming, or rolling. *See also* personal flotation device.

Canoe A small craft propelled with one or more single-bladed paddle(s), while sitting or kneeling and facing the direction of travel.

Canoeist A person who is competent at paddling a canoe.

Capsize To turn upside down in a boat.

Centre line Imaginary longitudinal line running through the boat from the bow to the stern.

Composite Made from a combination of more than one material, usually resin and a fabric (like carbon fibre).

Cross-bow Any stroke that is performed on one side of the boat using the paddle-blade normally reserved for the other side.

Deck The top of an enclosed boat; another word for spraydeck or skirt.

Delta Triangular type rig.

Depth The distance from the floor to the height of the gunwale measured at the boat's centre line.

Downstream Towards the sea.

Draft The vertical distance from the waterline of the boat to the lowest point of the boat.

Draw stroke A stroke that pulls the boat sideways through the water.

Drop Any pronounced change in the water level.

Dry-top A special type of cagoule designed for paddling, which has efficient seals to keep the water out.

Eddy An area of slack water moving upstream.

End grabs Handles at each end of a boat for use when carrying or towing the boat.

Falls Any distinct drop in the river level, but most often a vertical or near-vertical step down.

Feather To angle a paddle blade; the term usually refers to the angle between the two blades of a kayak paddle (an angle of between 30° and 90°).

Feedback (from the water) Kinaesthetic awareness of forces acting on you, the boat or the paddle.

Ferry glide A technique for crossing a current without moving up- or down-stream.

Flare The amount the sides of a canoe curve outward from the perpendicular; can also mean an illuminating safety device that can be used by paddlers in distress to attract attention at sea.

Flat water Water that does not have waves or currents that are strong enough to affect a canoe or kayak.

Flotation Material encased beneath the bow and stern decks that allows the canoe to float when swamped.

Forward Toward the bow of the boat.

Forward sweep stroke The most basic form of turning stroke, which can be used while the boat is stationary or in motion.

Free blade Any paddle or propulsion device that is held in the hands and not attached to the boat.

Freeboard The distance between the waterline and the gunwale of the canoe.

Grade/grading The name given to the accepted system for describing the severity of rapids.

Green water Unaerated – but not necessarily flat – water.

Grip The way in which you hold the paddle, or the specific part of a paddle shaft that rests in the hand.

Gunwale A strengthening rail, running the length of the canoe on each side, which is attached to the top edge of the boat sides.

H or HI rescue A technique for emptying another person's boat with help from another boater, while afloat.

Hand-roll To right the capsized craft using only the hands, without having to get out.

High brace A more advanced support stroke that is to be avoided if possible since it carries a risk of injury.

Hull The underside of any type of boat.

Husky tow Two or more paddlers towing a third paddler who may be tired or injured and experiencing difficulty on their own.

J-stroke A special canoe stroke that keeps the boat travelling in a straight line without the need to paddle on both sides.

Kayak A small craft propelled with one or more two-bladed paddle(s) while sitting and facing the direction of travel.

Kayaker A person who is competent at paddling a kayak.

Keel A longitudinal V-shape to the boat's bottom, on its centre line, to give strength, protection, and added control.

Leeward From the boat, the direction toward which the wind is blowing.

Low brace A basic support stroke.

Oar A paddle-like propulsion device that is attached to a boat when in use.

Offside The side of the canoe opposite that on which the blade is normally used.

Onside The side on which a canoe is normally paddled (left or right according to personal preference).

Open water A large expanse of usually flat water, typically a sea, lake, or very large river.

Paddler Common generic term for a canoeist or kayaker.

PFD (personal flotation device) US description of a buoyancy aid or lifejacket.

Pin spot A place where there is a natural danger of physical entrapment.

Pocket/Power Pocket The steepest green part of the wave, usually right next to the shoulder.

Pontoon A tethered, floating platform.

Port The left side of the boat as you face forward.

Portage The carrying of a boat or its contents over land from one body of water to another.

Prys Strokes that are performed by levering the paddle shaft against the side of the boat (usually a canoe).

Rapid An area of turbulent water.

Recirculate To be repeatedly carried upstream and submerged by the towback of a hydraulic water feature, such as a stopper wave.

Reverse sweep stroke A basic turning stroke that can be used while the boat is stationary or on the move.

Ribs Frames on the inside or outside of the hull to give additional strength.

Rocker The amount a boat's hull appears to be curved upwards at the ends.

Roll To right a craft after a capsize without having to get out.

Saddle An open canoe seat that is straddled by the paddler.

Sculling Imparting a force using a continuous to and fro action with a submerged blade.

Sculling draw A technique that propels the boat continuously sideways towards the paddle.

Sculling pry Like a sculling draw, but the pry propels the boat sideways away from the paddle.

Seal launch To slide or drop into the water while seated in the boat and holding the paddle.

Seams Where two currents converge they often fold downwards to make a seam-like feature on the surface.

Shaft The cylindrical part of the paddle, also known as the loom.

Shoulder The edge of the breaking part of a wave.

Shuttle The vehicle used for, or the practice of, transporting paddlers or equipment by road to the opposite end of a paddling trip.

Siphon Anywhere the current goes under an obstruction, such as a tree, with no airspace.

Ski A sit-on-top surf craft.

Skirt *See* spraydeck.

Smiley Any hydraulic with the ends (and hence the exits) downstream of, or lower than, the middle of the hydraulic.

Spraydeck (spray skirt) A device that is worn around the waist to keep water out of the cockpit.

Spray rail Longitudinal rails running slightly above the waterline on the outside, to deflect waves and chop.

Starboard The right-hand side of the boat as you face forward.

Stern The rearmost end of the canoe.

Stern paddler Paddler seated in the rear of the boat (kayak or canoe).

Stern rudder A steering stroke to be used while moving forwards.

Stopper A retentive (recirculating) wave capable of stopping and holding a boat, swimmer or any buoyant object hitting it from upstream (also known as a hole).

Strainer An obstruction through which the water is forced, forming a sieve-like effect.

Symmetrical Of a paddle, that the blades are a symmetrical shape; it does not mean that the blades are the same.

Tandem paddling Two paddlers paddling the same boat.

T-grip The handle on top of a canoe paddle shaft.

Throwline A proprietary rescue device carried by most whitewater paddlers.

Thwart A support or seat extending across width of canoe from gunwale to gunwale.

To ship water To accidentally take on water.

Touring Travelling the countryside by boat.

Towline A proprietary rescue device commonly used by instructors.

Tracking The term used to describe how well a boat tracks (keeps its direction) under the influence of currents and wind.

Transom The square stern in canoes designed for stern-mounted outboards.

Trim To load the boat so that it is level or slightly stern-down.

Trimming Making the boat float level by redistributing the weight of paddlers or gear.

Tumblehome The amount the sides of a canoe curve out and then return inward from the perpendicular.

Upstream Towards the source of the river.

Volume The amount of air trapped inside a boat; also refers to the volume of water moving down a rapid.

Wave-wheel A cartwheel-type manoeuvre performed going down the back of a wave.

Wet exit The procedure for bailing out from the boat while under water, following a capsize.

Whirlpools Whirling vertical vortices with a core of air that carry anything that falls into them down to the bed of the river, lake or sea. Similar to the way in which water swirls down the plughole of a bath.

White water Water that, because of the wind or the current, has become turbulent enough to become aerated and appears white and frothy.

Wilderness paddling Paddling far away from the resources of civilization.

Windage The degree to which a boat's sides are exposed to, or tend to catch, the wind.

Windward From the boat, the direction from which the wind is blowing.

X-rescue A technique for emptying another person's boat single-handed while afloat.

Useful Addresses

National Governing Bodies

British Canoe Union
Dudderidge House
Adbolton Lane
West Bridgford
Nottingham NG2 5AS
United Kingdom

American Canoe Association
8580 Cinderbed Road
Suite 1900
Newington
Virginia
United States

Canadian Canoe Association
333 River Road
Vanier City
Ontario K1L 8B9
Canada

Australian Canoe Federation
Room 510 Sports House
157 Gloucester Street
Sydney
NSW 2000
Australia

New Zealand Canoe Association
P. O. Box 3768
Wellington
New Zealand

French Canoe Kayak Federation
17 Route de Vienne
69007 Lyon
France

German Canoe Association
Berta-allee 8
4100 Duisberg 1
Germany

Training and Education

United Kingdom
Royal Lifesaving Society
Mounbatten House
Studley
Warwickshire B80 7NN
United Kingdom
Tel: (01789) 773 994

British Waterways
Melbury House
Melbury Terrace
London NW1 6JX

International Long River Canoeist Club
Catalina Cottage
Aultvullin
Strathay Point
Sutherland
KW14 7RY

Advanced Sea Kayak Club
7 Miller Close
Newport
Isle of Wight
PO30 5PS

For details of canoe and kayak clubs in your area, please contact the British Canoe Union.

United States
Rescue 3 International
9075 Elk Grove Boulevard 200
P. O. Box 519
Elk Grove
California 95759-0519
Tel: (916) 685 3066
Customer Support 800–45–RESCU
www.rescue3.com

American Rivers
801 Pennsylvania Ave S. E. Suite 303
Washington DC 20003

Nantahala Outdoor Center
US 19W Box 41
Bryson City
NC 28713
Tel: (704) 488 2175

A directory of state and local clubs can be found in the *ACA Canoeing and Kayaking Instruction Manual.*

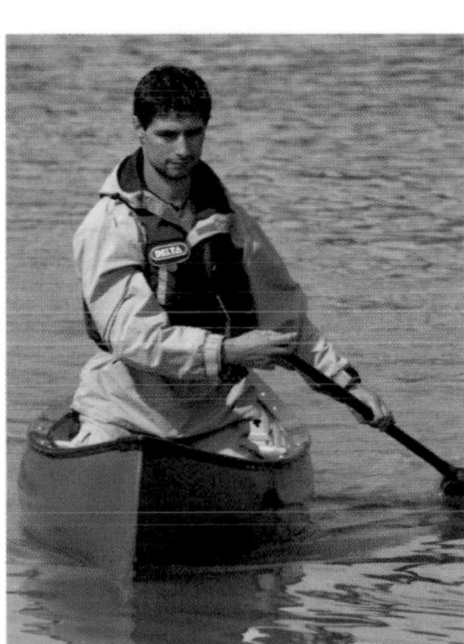

Further Reading

Books

Canoeing: A Trailside Guide
Gordon Grant/Norton (1997)

Outdoor Pursuits Series: Canoeing
Laurie Gullion/Human Kinetics Publishers (1994)

The Canoe Handbook
Slim Ray/Stackpole Books (1992)

Canoeing Handbook
Edited by Ray Rowe/British Canoe Union (1997)

Teach Yourself Canoeing
Ray Rowe/Hodder & Stoughton (1992)

Kayaking: White Water and Touring Basics/Trailside Guides
Steven M. Krauzer/Norton (1995)

Kayak: The Animated Manual of Intermediate and Advanced Whitewater Technique
William Nealy/Cordee (1990)

White Water Kayaking
Ray Rowe/Hodder & Stoughton (1988)

Sea Kayaking
John Dowd/Douglas & MacIntyre (1988)

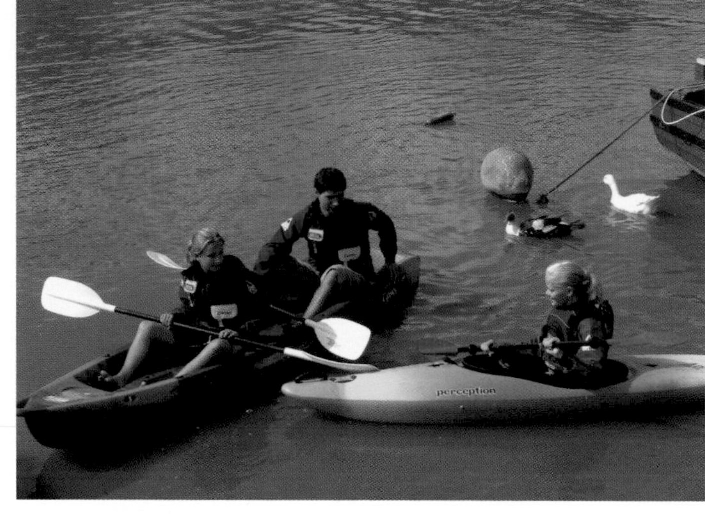

Squirt Boating and Beyond
James E. Snyder/Menasha Ridge Press (2001)

The Art of Freestyle
Brymer, Hughes and Collins/Pesda Press (2000)

Weather Forecasting for Sailors
Frank Singleton/Hodder & Stoughton (1981)

Magazines

Canoe Kayak and **Playboating**
Gunn Publishing
179 Bath Road, Cheltenham
United Kingdon GL53 7LY
Tel: (01242) 539 390

Paddles
Alexander House,
Ling Road,
Poole, Dorset,
United Kingdom BH12 4NZ
Tel: (01202) 735 090

Canoe & Kayak
10526 NE 68th Street,
Suite 3, Kirkland,
WA 98033,
United States
Tel:(800) 829 3340

The American Canoeist
P. O. Box 1190,
Newington,
Virginia 22122
United States

Kayak Session
3 Rue de la Claire
69009 Lyon
France
Tel: (472) 19 87 97

Index

ACADIA

ACADIA

Acknowledgements

The author, photographer and publishers would like to thank the following individuals for their valuable contributions to this book:

Kevin Andriessen, Pete Astles, Dragons Alive Team Activity Group, Duncan Eades, Nathan Eades, Rob Feloy, Rodney Forte, Paul Grogan, Dino Heald, Darren James, Graham Mackereth, Malcolm at Mega Kayaks, Mark Potts, Jason Smith and Martin Tapley.

Thanks also to the following companies who supplied clothing and equipment for photography:

AS Watersports
Kayaking and canoeing accessories.

Delta Sportswear Ltd
www.delta-sportswear.com
Kayaking and canoeing clothing accessories.

Nookie Xtreme Sports Equipment
Kayaking clothing, accessories and safety equipment.
www.nookie.co.uk

Perception Kayaks
www.perception.co.uk

Pyranha Mouldings Ltd
Canoes and kayaks.

River Dart Country Park
For photography locations, logistics, hospitality and bank support.

System X
Werner and Schlegel paddles.

Thanks also to the following models, canoeists and kayakers:

Alec Ashmore, Steve Balcombe, Nikki Ball, Duncan Browne, Owen Davies, David Dean, Tim Denson, Rob Feloy, Mark Harvey, Roger Hopper, Mariano Kälfors, Beki King, Tom Klamfor, David Manlow, Bill Mattos, Tim Maud, Jon Miles, Lee Pritchard, Jason Scholey, J. Simpson, Howard Smith, Tank, James Weir, Steve Whetman, Hazel Wilson and Paul Woodward.

Picture Credits
All photography by Helen Metcalfe except for the following.
t = top; b = bottom; c = centre; l = left; r = right

The Art Archive 12t, 12b.
Dino Heald 28bl.
Mark Potts 31tr.
Dan Trotter 115b.

Notes

Notes

Notes

Notes